Tom H

hotline

starter

student's book

OXFORD UNIVERSITY PRESS

Oxford University Press
Walton Street, Oxford OX2 6DP

Oxford New York
Athens Auckland Bangkok Bombay
Calcutta Cape Town Dar es Salaam Delhi
Florence Hong Kong Istanbul Karachi
Kuala Lumpur Madras Madrid Melbourne
Mexico City Nairobi Paris Singapore
Taipei Tokyo Toronto

and associated companies in
Berlin Ibadan

Oxford and Oxford English are trade marks of Oxford
University Press

First published 1991
Fifteenth impression 1997

ISBN 0 19 435481 4

Acknowledgements

The author would like to thank Suzanna Harsányi (Editorial
Manager) and John Raby (Senior Editor) for their tireless
efforts in turning manuscript into published work. Thanks
are also due to all the people at Oxford University Press
who have contributed their skills and ideas to producing
this book. Thanks are due in particular to Pearl Bevan
(Senior Design Project Manager), Katy Wheeler (Art
Editor), Elana Katz (Freelance Editor), Fran Holdsworth
(Freelance Designer), Keith Shaw (Freelance Designer),
Pippa Mayfield (Editor), Amanda Goodridge (Designer),
and Malcolm Price (Production).

The author would especially like to record his gratitude to
his wife Pamela and his children, without whose support
and patience Hotline would not have been possible.

The publishers would like to thank all of the ELT teachers
and advisers around the world who have given generously
of their time to talk about their needs and to comment on
the manuscript and sample units of Hotline. Our thanks are
especially due to:

Silvia Ronchetti (Instituto Superior del Profesorado en
Lenguas Vivas, Buenos Aires) in Argentina. Freddy Désir
(Inspection de l'Enseignement Secondaire de l'Etat,
Brussels), Norbert Jacquinet (Institut Notre-Dame,
Brussels) in Belgium. Edit Nagy (National Institute of
Education, Budapest), Lyane Szentirmay (Madách Imre
Gimnázium, Budapest), Judit Sióréti (Városmajori
Gimnázium, Budapest), Ilona Jobbágy (Könyves Kálmán
Gimnázium, Budapest) in Hungary. Orazio Marchi
(Progetto Speciale Lingue Straniere, Forlì) in Italy. Diana
England and Monica Green (International House, Lisbon)
in Portugal. Patsy Fuller (Freelance Teacher), Luis
Fernández (I.B. Alexandre Satorras, Mataro), Vincenc Haro
and Merce Fosch (I.B. Ferran Casablanca, Sabadell),
Eleanor Tompkins (La Salle Congres, Barcelona), Ana Coll
(I.B. Narcis Monturiol, Barcelona), Victoria Alcalde (I.B.
San Isidro, Madrid), Joaquin Rojo (I.B. Francisco de Goya,
Madrid), Pedro Horillo and Margarita Hernández (I.B.
Verdaguer Parc de la Ciutadella, Barcelona), Pilar Gómez

(Instituto Cid Campeador, Valencia), María Jesús Marín (I.B.
Grande Cobián, Zaragoza), Santiago Remacha (I.B. La Jota,
Zaragoza) in Spain. Carroll Klein (Koç Özel Lisesi, Istanbul)
in Turkey.

Special thanks are due to a panel of British teenagers, Juliet
Kinsman, Zuleika Melluish, Pema Radha, Alex Huskinson
and Mark Killingley, who advised on the Victoria Road
storyline and on the Reading and Listening topics and to
whom we are indebted for the natural, colloquial teenage
language of the Victoria Road characters.

'Be-bop-a-lula', words and music by Gene Vincent and T.
Davis, used by kind permission of Carlin Music
Corporation, Iron Bridge House, 3 Bridge Approach, Chalk
Farm, London, NW1 8BD.

'Save me', words by John Raby.

The publishers and the author would like to thank the
following for their kind permission to use extracts from
copyright materials:

Guinness Publishing Ltd.: two facts from the Guinness
Book of Records. Copyright © 1983 Guinness Superlatives
Ltd. Octopus Publishing Group: extract from It can't be true
by Jane Reid.

Illustrations by:

Kevin Baverstock, Terry Beard, Roger Fereday/Linda
Rogers, Robina Green, Nick Harris, Leo Hartas, Nick
Hawken, Jonathon Heap, Ian Heard, Stephen Holmes,
Conny Jude, Michael Kumon, Dave Murray, Savicis
Neocleous, Denis Ryan/Artists Partners, Tech Graphics.

The publishers would like to thank the following for their
permission to reproduce photographs:

Ace/Mauritius Bildagentur; Action Plus/Chris Barry, Mike
Hewitt; Allsport/David Cannon; Aquarius Picture Library;
Capital Radio; J.A. Cash; Colorific/Frank Herman, Duncan
Raban/All Action, Anthony Suan Black; Star 1987;
Colorsport; Greg Evans; Mary Evans Picture Library;
Feature Pix; Fortean Picture Library; Sally and Richard
Greenhill; Robert Harding; Hulton Deutsch Collection;
Image Bank/Inone, Elaine Sulle, P. Tesman; Looks
Magazine/Steve Cartwright; Niall McInerney; Mizz
Holiday Special/Mike Prior; Palace/Aquarius; Retna/Jenny
Acheson, Tammy Arroyd, E.J. Camp, Sam Emerson/Onyx,
Gary Gershoff, Adrian Green, Trevor Leighton, C.L.
Kirsch, Greg Noakes, Steve Rapport, Paul Rider, Paul
Slattery, Chris VD Vooren; Rex Features/Brendan Beirne,
D. Graves, Nils Jorgensen, Levenson; D.C. Thomson and
Co. Ltd; Universal/Aquarius; Elizabeth Whiting Associates.

Victoria Road photography by John Walmsley.

Stills photography by Rob Judges.

Studio photography by Martyn Chillmaid, Paul Freestone,
Mark Mason, Garry and Marilyn O'Brien.

The characters in Victoria Road were played by:

Sarah Buckley, Matthew Christmas, Joseph Derrett, Natalie
Kowlessur, Tito Menezes, Robert Page, Graham and Sue
Page, Simon Richards, Paul and Pat Rose, Sarah Rose,
Patrick Short, Matthew Starling.

The publishers would like to thank the following for their
help with the Victoria Road photo story:

Ardmore Adventure Holidays; Banstead Sports Centre;
Cannon cinema, Ewell; Epsom and Ewell High School;
London and Country Buses; McDonalds; Met Police Public
Relations; Mrs Moretta; Frances Myers; NESCOT drama
department; One Stop Shop, Burgh Heath; Pickfords; St
Andrews School, Leatherhead; St David's School, Ashford;
Therfield School, Leatherhead; Thorndike Youth Theatre;
Rose and Brian Walsh; Whitgift Centre, Croydon;
Worcester Park Football Club.

What's your name?

1 📼 **Listen.**

Hello. My name's Sonia. I'm from Britain.

Hi. I'm Jason Donovan. I'm from Australia. What's your name?

2 **Listen again and repeat.**

3 **Work with your classmates. Ask and answer.**

> Example
> **A** 'Hello, I'm Maria. What's your name?'
> **B** 'My name's Carlo.'

FOLLOW UP

4 **Introduce yourself.**

Hi. My name's Julia. I'm from Italy.

Who's this?

1 Match the names of the people to the places.

☒ Cory Aquino ─────────
☐ Mikhail Gorbachev
☐ Arancha Sanchez
☐ Nelson Piquet
☐ Tina Turner
☐ Boris Becker
☐ Princess Diana
☐ Diego Maradona
☐ Kylie Minogue

☐ the USSR
H the Philippines
☐ the USA
☐ Britain
☐ Argentina
☐ Brazil
☐ Australia
☐ Spain
☐ Germany

2 Write about the people.

Example
This is Cory Aquino. She's from the Philippines.
This is Mikhail Gorbachev. He's from . . . .

5

6

3

4

2

1

9

8

7

A grammar rule

 Short and long forms

Look.

short form	long form
I'm Jason Donovan. =	**I am** Jason Donovan.
She's from Spain. =	**She is** from Spain.

Complete these with the long form.

He's Boris Becker.   =   He .... Boris Becker.

I'm from Greece.   =   I .... from Greece.

My name's Sonia.   =   My name .... Sonia.

What's your name? =   What .... your name?

A GAME

 Choose one of the famous people. Introduce yourself to the class.

    Example
Hello, I'm Princess Di. I'm from Britain.

FOLLOW UP

Introduce your favourite pop star and your favourite sports star.

    Example

This is Michael Jackson. He's from the United States.

My favourite pop star.

This is Gabriela Sabatini. She's from Argentina.

My favourite sports star.

Some useful words

Look at the picture. Find the missing words in this list.

desk   pen   blackboard   bag   door
window   teacher   pencil   book
cassette recorder

Check your answers with your teacher or a dictionary.

Fast Cars

The alphabet

1 📼 Listen and repeat.

A B C D E F G H I
J K L M N O P Q R
S T U V W X Y Z

2 a Look at these cars. Do you know their names?

b Here are their names. They are all mixed up.

S   XJS   T-Bar   MR2
VW   MG   TVR   GTI
XR3i   BGT

c 📼 Listen and write the names below the cars.

3 Ask and answer.

Example
A 'What's this?'
B 'It's a TVR S Convertible.'

4 Which car do you like best? What is the most popular car in the class?

Numbers 0–10

5 📼 Listen and repeat.

0	1	2	3	4	5
zero (oh)	one	two	three	four	five

6	7	8	9	10
six	seven	eight	nine	ten

A GAME

6 How good is your memory? Work with a partner. Look at the cars for one minute.

A Read one of the number plates.
B (book closed) Write the number. Say which car it is.

Example
A 'A four two nine B T H.'
B 'It's the VW Golf.'

1 ....
RKP 794X

2 Toyota ....

3 .... Convertible
F836 DWN

4 .... Golf ....
A429 BTH

5 Jaguar ....
C20 4 MIU

6 Ford Escort .... Cabriolet
LEQ 317Y

FOLLOW UP

7 Write these numbers in full.

Example
   0   1   7   5   9   8   3   2   4
zero

Radio 581

1 a Look at the dialogue.

b Listen and complete it.

DJ This .... the Hotline programme on Radio 581. .... Candy Jones and Steve Turner is on the line. .... , Steve.

Steve Hi.

DJ Who is .... record for, Steve?

Steve It's for .... girlfriend, Kate. .... her birthday today.

DJ Happy .... , Kate. How old is .... ?

Steve Oh, I don't know. .... sixteen, I think.

DJ Thank you, Steve. Now for Steve .... his girlfriend, Kate, here's Donna Summer.

2 Work with a partner. Read the dialogue.

Numbers 11–20

3 Listen and match the numbers to the correct words.

11	thirteen
12	sixteen
13	fourteen
14	eighteen
15	eleven
16	nineteen
17	twenty
18	twelve
19	seventeen
20	fifteen

Make a rule: his / her

4 Complete these sentences. Write 'his' or 'her'.

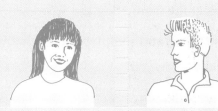

...... name's Kate.

It's ...... birthday today.

...... name's Steve.

Kate is ...... girlfriend.

Translate these sentences. Is the rule the same in your language?

When do we use 'his'? When do we use 'her'?

5 a Here are some sentences. Write 'his' or 'her'.

1 My record is for my girlfriend. .... name's Kate.

2 This record is for Michael and .... girlfriend.

3 My record is for my boyfriend. It's .... birthday today.

4 This record is for my girlfriend. It's .... birthday.

5 This record is for Kate and .... boyfriend.

b You are the DJ. Your partner is on the line. He/She wants a record for someone. Make the dialogue.

FOLLOW UP

6 Write the dialogue from Exercise 5b.

7

Fast food

Numbers 20 – 100

1 a Listen and repeat.

21	twenty-one	30	thirty
22	twenty-two	40	forty
23	twenty-three	50	fifty
24	twenty-four	60	sixty
25	twenty-five	70	seventy
26	twenty-six	80	eighty
27	twenty-seven	90	ninety
28	twenty-eight	100	a hundred
29	twenty-nine		

b **Count from thirty to sixty.**

c **Say these numbers in full.**

65   97   56   83   71   44   32

2 a **Look at the menu. Say the words.**

b **Listen and complete the dialogues.**

Can .... help you?

A .... and an ....,
please.

Anything else?

No, thank you.

That's £1.19, ...

....

Can I help you?

An .... and ....

Anything else?

Yes, a .... , please.

That's £........ , please.

Thank you.

3 **Work with a partner. Read the dialogues.**

Fat Cat Cafe

Apple juice **54p**

Cola **55p**

Orange juice **56p**

Hamburger **65p**

Eggburger **80p**

Cheeseburger **75p**

French fries **60p**

a / an

4 a Look.

a	an
a hamburger	**an** apple juice
a cola	**an** orange juice
	an eggburger

b When do we use 'a'? When do we use 'an'?
Explain the rule in your own language.

c Add these words to the correct list.

pen	apple	girlfriend
desk	bag	record
orange	egg	umbrella

5 Look at the menu. Make new dialogues.

FOLLOW UP

6 Write one of your dialogues from Exercise 5.

Asking for help

Practise these expressions.

What's this called?

What does .... mean?

How do you say .... in English?

How do you pronounce .... ?

How do you spell .... ?

2 you

to be

Contents

1 a 📼 **Listen and write the names in the correct places.**

Vince Kamala Sue Casey Terry Kam

Victoria Road Rap

My name's .... , ... Moore.

And this is .... , the girl next door.

Hi there, kids. My name's ....

Pleased to meet you. How do you do?

Chorus
Victoria Road, Victoria Road, Victoria Road,
   rap, rap, rap.
Victoria Road, Victoria Road, Victoria Road,
   rap, rap, rap.

Hi. I'm .... I'm her brother.

Terry's my friend. And here's another.

.... Royston is my name.

Football is my favourite game.

Chorus
Victoria Road, Victoria Road, Victoria Road,
   rap, rap, rap.
Victoria Road, Victoria Road, Victoria Road,
   rap, rap, rap.

.... is who I am.

But you're my friend. So call me ....

We're from Hartfield. Where are you from?

Add your name and sing our song.

Chorus
Victoria Road, Victoria Road, Victoria Road,
   rap, rap, rap.
Victoria Road, Victoria Road, Victoria Road,
   rap, rap, rap.

b **Look at the story on page 12. Check your answers.**

c **Now complete the names.**

.... Moore   .... Scott

.... Royston   .... Scott

.... Wijeratne

FOLLOW UP

2 Write a rhyme for your name and add it to the song.

Work out the meaning

1 What do you think these words mean? Look through the story. Make a guess.

brother   sister   friend   neighbour
boy   girl   twins

Check your ideas with your teacher or a dictionary.

2 🔊 Listen and follow in your books.

Sue Hi, are you our new neighbour? What's your name?

Terry Terry Moore. I . . .

Sue I'm Sue. This is my brother, Vince. We're twins.

Terry Oh, hel . . .

Sue Say hello, Vince. And this is his friend, Casey.

Kamala Hi, Sue.

Sue That's my best friend. Her name's Kamala.

Sue See you. Bye.

Terry Goodbye.

Later

Mrs Moore How old are the boy and girl next door?

Terry They're fifteen. They're twins.

Mrs Moore Oh, what are their names?

Terry Vince and Sue.

Mrs Moore What are they like?

Terry Vince is all right, but his sister's bossy.

Sue Huh. I'm not bossy. You just wait, Terry Moore!

3 Listen again and repeat.

> Hi. Are you our new neighbour? What's your name?

> Terry Moore. I...

1

> This is my brother, Vince. We're twins.

> Oh, hel....

2

> Hi, Sue.

> That's my best friend. Her name's Kamala.

3

How old are the boy and girl next door?

They're fifteen.

4

What are they like?

Vince is all right, but his sister's bossy.

5

A grammar table: 'to be'

6 We can use a table to show a grammar rule. This is a table. Complete it with these words.

She   's   are   'm   're   It   is   We

I	am	
	....	
He		from England.
......	....	
......	....	15.
......	....	in the garden.
	....	
You	....	
They		

Huh. I'm not bossy. You just wait, Terry Moore!

6

Useful expressions

4 How do you say these expressions in your language?

See you.

How old are . . .?

What are they like?

He's all right.

She's bossy.

You just wait!

5 Work in a group of 3. One person is Terry, one is Sue, one is all the other people. Read the story.

FOLLOW UP

7 Kamala is talking to Sue. Complete their conversation.

Kamala Hi, Sue.

Sue ...., Kam.

Kamala Is that boy your new

.... ?

Sue Yes, ... is.

Kamala What's .... name?

Sue Terry ....

Kamala How .... is he?

Sue .... fifteen.

Kamala What's he ....?

Sue He's a bit quiet, ... he's all

....

READING

Are you a Bros fan?....

> They're my favourite pop group.

> They're rubbish.

> They're all right.

> They aren't very good.

1 a Look at these pop stars. Do you know them?

b Read what people say about them.

> She's OK.

> She's great!

> She's awful.

> She isn't my favourite singer.

> He's wonderful.

> He isn't bad.

> I'm not a Michael Jackson fan.

> He's terrible.

2 Now listen. Which pop star are they talking about?

Example
He isn't bad.
It's Michael Jackson.

3 What do you think of these people? Use the expressions above.

The verb 'to be': negative

BUILD UP

4 a Look. Complete the sentences.

I .... a Michael Jackson fan.

She .... my favourite singer.

They .... very good.

b Complete the table.

I	am not 'm not	
		bad.
He She It	....	very good.
		rubbish.
We You They	....	

5 Make true sentences by completing these.

a I .... from America.

b Michael Jackson .... my favourite pop star.

c My parents .... millionaires.

d Our English teacher .... bossy.

e I .... a girl.

f I .... a boy.

g The Beatles .... terrible.

h English .... my favourite subject.

i My partner and I .... the best students in the class.

6 Who are your favourite pop stars? Do other people like them? Ask them.

FOLLOW UP

7 Choose six pop stars or pop groups. Write your opinion of each one.

LISTENING

 1 **Terry is joining the Hartfield leisure centre.**

📼 **Listen and complete his form.**

Hartfield Leisure Centre

Membership Card No: **694/M**

Name: ....

Age: ....

Address: ....

Telephone number: ....

The verb 'to be': questions

BUILD UP

2 **a** **Complete the questions.**

Example
Vince and Sue ⟍are⟋ twins.

Are⟍ Vince and Sue⟋ twins?

Sue is in the kitchen.

.... in the kitchen?

You are fifteen.

.... fifteen?

He's from Spain.

.... from Spain?

---
b **How do we make questions with 'to be'?**
Explain in your own language.
---

 3 **Mr Moore is asking Terry some questions.**
Use these cues. Make the questions.

Example
Vince / our neighbour
Is Vince our neighbour?

Sue / his sister
they / twins
they / all right
they / sixteen
Casey / their friend
he / fifteen, too
Kamala and Casey / our neighbours, too
Kamala / your friend

 4 **a** **Listen again and complete the dialogue.**

Woman ....?

Terry Terry Moore.

Woman ....?

Terry M double O R E.

Woman .... Are you 16?

Terry No, I'm not. I'm 15.

Woman .... address?

Terry 20 Victoria Road, Hartfield.

Woman .... telephone

.............................?

Terry 732983.

Woman Welcome to the leisure centre, Terry.
That's £5.50, please.

b **Work with a partner. Read the dialogue.**

 5 **Interview your partner. Complete his/her card.**

Hartfield Leisure Centre

Membership Card No: ....

Name: ....

Age: ....

Address: ....

Telephone number: ....

FOLLOW UP

6 **Make a membership card for yourself. Write your dialogue for Exercise 5.**

INTERACTION

At the shops

1 a Make the dialogue. Put each sentence in the correct speech bubble.

That's 40p, please.
That's £5.40 altogether, please.
Thank you.
It's £5.
Here you are.
How much are these postcards?
And how much is this yellow T-shirt?
Thank you.
I'll take it, please.
Can I have these four, please?
The small postcards are 10p each and the large
    postcards are 15p each.
That's 60p change.

b 🔊 Listen and check your answer.

c Practise the dialogue in pairs.

16

Plurals

 a Look.

a postcard  four postcards

a T-shirt two T-shirts

b How do we make the plural?
Explain in your own language.

this / these

 a Complete these with 'this' or 'these'.

....
green T-shirt  postcards

b Complete these sentences.

> Example
> *How much are these red apples?*

How much .... red apples?

How much .... radio?

How much .... watches?

How much .... badges?

How much .... green umbrella?

How much .... cassette recorder?

How much .... pens?

Adjective and noun

 a Look.

the **small** postcards   this **green** T-shirt
the **large** postcards   these **red** apples

b Where is the adjective?

c Translate them. Is it the same in your language?

 Describe these things. Use these words.

red   yellow   **blue**   **green**

white   **black**   small   **large**

 Look at the pictures above. Make dialogues. Use the dialogue in Exercise 1 as a model.

A You are a customer. Buy two things from the shop.
B You are the sales assistant.

FOLLOW UP

Write one of your dialogues from Exercise 6.

PROJECT

You

Here's your first project. Make a project about YOU.

- Give some information about yourself.
- Show some of your favourite things.

Use Vince's project as a model.

This is my House
My Address is
58 Victoria Road
Hartfield

This is Terry
He's our Neighbour

Casey

My ★ FRIENDS

This is my sister

Sue we're Twins

These are my friends in the garden

RING

0386754921

Great

My name's
Vince Scott. I'm
from Hartfield in
England.
I'm 15.

my favourite T-Shirt

Learning diary

A Look at the first page of this unit. How well do you know these things now? Look at each point in the contents list.

If you know it well, draw a happy face.

If you know it fairly well, draw a face like this.

If you don't know it well, draw a sad face.

B Try the self-check in the Workbook.

C Compare your answers with a partner. Discuss any problems with your teacher.

2

▶ Pronunciation: page 111

3 people

have/has got

Contents

Grammar points

The main grammar point in this unit is:

have / has got

> I have got fair hair.
> I have got blue eyes.
> I haven't got dark hair.
> What colour hair have you got?

Kamala has got black hair.
She has got brown eyes.
She hasn't got blond hair.
Has she got blue eyes?

Terry's date

1 Look at the story.

- Who are the people?
- Where are they?
- What are they talking about?
- Who are:
  Jane Fox
  Darren Tooley?

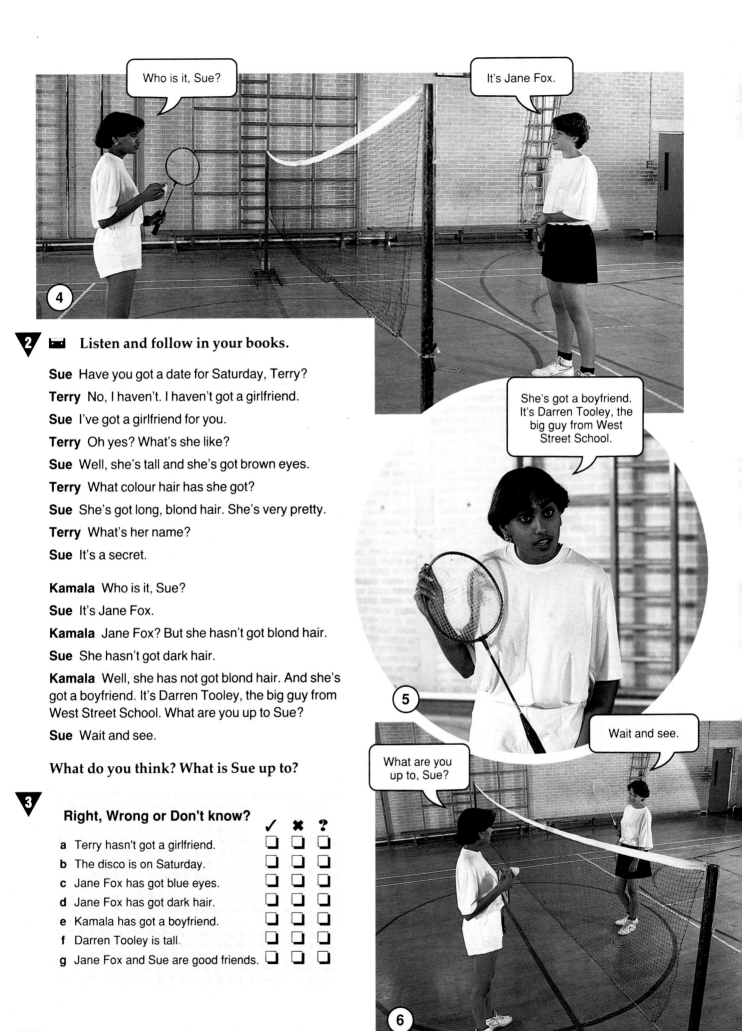

2 📼 **Listen and follow in your books.**

Sue Have you got a date for Saturday, Terry?

Terry No, I haven't. I haven't got a girlfriend.

Sue I've got a girlfriend for you.

Terry Oh yes? What's she like?

Sue Well, she's tall and she's got brown eyes.

Terry What colour hair has she got?

Sue She's got long, blond hair. She's very pretty.

Terry What's her name?

Sue It's a secret.

Kamala Who is it, Sue?

Sue It's Jane Fox.

Kamala Jane Fox? But she hasn't got blond hair.

Sue She hasn't got dark hair.

Kamala Well, she has not got blond hair. And she's got a boyfriend. It's Darren Tooley, the big guy from West Street School. What are you up to Sue?

Sue Wait and see.

What do you think? What is Sue up to?

3

Right, Wrong or Don't know?

	✓	✗	?
a Terry hasn't got a girlfriend.	☐	☐	☐
b The disco is on Saturday.	☐	☐	☐
c Jane Fox has got blue eyes.	☐	☐	☐
d Jane Fox has got dark hair.	☐	☐	☐
e Kamala has got a boyfriend.	☐	☐	☐
f Darren Tooley is tall.	☐	☐	☐
g Jane Fox and Sue are good friends.	☐	☐	☐

4 **Listen again and repeat.**

Useful expressions

5 How do you say these in your language?

Have you got a date?

I haven't got a girlfriend.

What is she like?

What colour hair has she got?

It's a secret.

She's got a boyfriend.

a big guy

What are you up to?

Wait and see.

have / has got

BUILD UP

6 **a** Look at the story, and the examples on page 19 again. Find these incomplete sentences and complete them.

I .... fair hair.

I............................ a girlfriend for you.

I have not got blue eyes.

I .... a girlfriend.

Kamala .... got black hair.

She............................ long, blond hair.

Well, she .... blond hair.

She .... dark hair.

b Now complete this table.

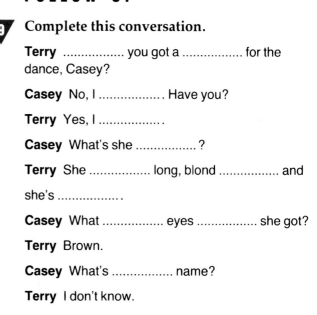

7 Write true sentences. Use 'have', 'has', 'haven't' or 'hasn't'.

a Jane Fox .... got brown eyes.

b Sue .... got a secret.

c Terry .... got a girlfriend.

d Kamala and Casey .... got black hair.

e Sue .... got a sister.

f Jane Fox .... got a boyfriend.

g I .... got short hair.

h My best friend .... got fair hair.

i I .... got three brothers.

j We .... got a fast car.

8 Work in a group of three. Each person takes one part. Read the story.

FOLLOW UP

9 Complete this conversation.

Terry .... you got a .... for the dance, Casey?

Casey No, I .... Have you?

Terry Yes, I ....

Casey What's she .... ?

Terry She .... long, blond .... and she's ....

Casey What .... eyes .... she got?

Terry Brown.

Casey What's .... name?

Terry I don't know.

READING

Genitives

BUILD UP

 1 Look.

Sue is **Vince's** sister.
Vince is **Sue's** brother.   sister   brother

 2 Look at the family below. Who are the people?

 3 What do these words mean?

husband	son	daughter
wife	grandson	parents
mother	grandmother	father

Read the clues. Use the diagram to find the meanings of these words.

Princess Bea's mother is called Fergie.
Prince Philip is the Queen's husband.
Princess Diana and Prince Charles have got two sons.
Princess Anne and Captain Mark Philips have got a son and a daughter.
Princess Diana is Prince Charles' wife.
The Queen is Prince William's grandmother.
The Queen and Prince Philip have got three grandsons.
Peter and Zara Philips' parents are Princess Anne and Captain Mark Philips.

Using a pattern

W O R D   W O R K

 4 Complete the list.

son	grandson
daughter	....
mother	grandmother
father	....
parents	....

5 Complete these sentences.

a Fergie is .... wife.
b Prince William is .... son.
c Prince Philip is Princess Bea's ....
d The Queen is Prince Edward's ....
e Prince Harry is .... brother.
f Prince Charles is .... husband.

The Queen = Prince Philip

Princess Diana = *Prince Charles*   *Princess Anne* = *Captain Mark Philips*   *The Duchess of York (Fergie)* = *Prince Andrew*   *Prince Edward*

Prince William *Prince Harry*   *Peter Philips* *Zara Philips*   *Princess Bea* *Princess Eugenie*

FOLLOW UP

 6 Describe a famous family from your country.

LISTENING

Blind Date

 1   Listen to the radio programme. What is it about?

2   Listen again and complete this chart.

	1	2	3
from			
hair			
eyes			
job			
favourite pop star			

3   Who does Angie choose?

- What do you think?

- Listen to the second part and find out.

a/an + job

4   a   Look.

    I'm **a** student.
    He's **an** engineer.

b   Compare this to your own language.

5   Use a dictionary.

a   Say what these people are.

b   What about your family? What are their jobs?

    Example
    My mother is a bank manager.

6   Work with a partner. Use your chart. Role play the radio show.

FOLLOW UP

7   Use your chart. Describe the three boys.

INTERACTION

have / has got: questions

BUILD UP

1 **a Complete these sentences.**

You have got a girlfriend.

.... a girlfriend?

She has got fair hair.

.... fair hair?

b Complete this table.

	I you we they			brown eyes?
....			....	blond hair?
....	he she it			a sister?

c How do we make questions with 'have / has got'? Explain in your own language.

2 **Work with a partner. Ask and answer these.**

Example
Have you got a brother?
Yes, I've got two brothers.

a brother	a boyfriend / girlfriend
a walkman	a best friend
a computer	a dictionary
a sister	a house or flat
a watch	a favourite record

YOUR RADIO SHOW

3 **a Look at the Blind Date show on page 24. Work in a group of five.**

b Make your own programme. Each person takes a part.

c Act your radio show.

FOLLOW UP

4 **Write one of the dialogues from your show.**

Your Blind Date File

You want to go on the Blind Date show. First we need some information about you.

We need a photograph.

And we need some basic information. Please answer these questions.

PUT YOUR PHOTOGRAPH HERE

What's your full name?
What do your friends call you?
Are you male or female?
How old are you?
Where are you from?
What colour eyes have you got?
What colour hair have you got?
How tall are you?

Your likes and dislikes

Now we'd like some information about your likes and dislikes.

Who's your favourite pop star?
Who's your least favourite pop star?
What's your favourite food?
What's your favourite colour?
What's your favourite TV programme?
What are your favourite things?
What's the worst thing in the world?

The opposite sex

Give us your ideas about the opposite sex.

Describe your ideal date.
Describe your least ideal date.

Yourself

Lastly, can we have your ideas about yourself?

Which of these do you think you are? Tick them.

good-looking ☐	fun ☐	happy ☐
interesting ☐	boring ☐	bossy ☐
intelligent ☐	friendly ☐	shy ☐
quiet ☐	nice ☐	honest ☐

PROJECT

My family

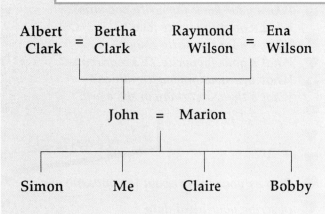

> This is my Mum.
> Her name's Marion.

> This is my Dad.
> His name's John.

> This is my
> little sister
> Claire.
> She's ten.

> This is my big
> brother, Simon.
> He's an
> architect.

> This is Simon's
> girlfriend. Her
> name's Julia.

> This is my little brother,
> Bobby. He's seven.

```
Albert   =  Bertha     Raymond  =  Ena
Clark       Clark      Wilson      Wilson
              |_____|
                        |
              John  =  Marion
                        |
        _____|_____
        |        |          |           |
      Simon     Me        Claire      Bobby
```

a Write about your family.

- Find a photograph of your family.
- Write some information about
  the people in your photograph.

  their names
  their relationships to you
  their jobs

b Draw a family tree for your family.

- Describe the people in your family tree.

  Example
  *My grandmother has got dark hair and brown
  eyes. She's tall.*

- Who do you look like in your family?

Learning diary

A Look at the first page of this unit.
How well do you know these things
now? Look at each point in the
contents list.

If you know it well,
draw a happy face.

If you know it fairly well,
draw a face like this.

If you don't know it well,
draw a sad face.

3

B Try the self-check in the Workbook.

C Compare your answers with a
partner. Discuss any
problems with your teacher.

can / can't; times

Contents

Grammar points

The main grammar point in this unit is:

can / can't

1 **Look at the story.**

- Who are the people?
- Where are they?
- What happens?

> Terry, can you see that girl over there? She's your date.

2 🔊 **Listen and follow in your books.**

Sue Terry, can you see that girl over there? She's your date.

Terry Where? I can't see a girl with blond hair.

Sue Well, her hair's fair really. She's over there near the door.

Terry Oh yes, I can see her.

Sue Well, go on, Terry.

Terry Er, excuse me. Would you like to dance?

Jane I . . . er . . . I'm sorry. I can't.

Terry What? Can't you dance? Everybody can dance.

Jane No, I mean, I . . . .

Darren Can't you hear, stupid? The answer is 'No'. All right?

Jane This is my boyfriend, Darren.

Terry Oh, er, sorry.

Sue Ha, ha, ha! Oh, Terry, your face. It's so funny.

> Excuse me. Would you like to dance?

> I... er... I'm sorry. I can't.

> What? Can't you dance? Everybody can dance.

Can't you hear, stupid? The answer is 'No'.

This is my boyfriend, Darren.

Oh, er, sorry.

Ha, ha, ha. Oh, Terry, your face. It's so funny.

Right, Wrong or Don't know?

		✓	✗	?
a	Sue, Kamala and Terry are at the dance.	❑	❑	❑
b	Kamala has got a date.	❑	❑	❑
c	Sue can't see Jane Fox.	❑	❑	❑
d	Jane Fox is near the window.	❑	❑	❑
e	Jane has got blond hair.	❑	❑	❑
f	Casey is at the dance.	❑	❑	❑
g	Jane's boyfriend isn't at the dance.	❑	❑	❑
h	Darren Tooley can't dance.	❑	❑	❑
i	Sue is pleased.	❑	❑	❑

4 Listen again and repeat.

Useful expressions

5 How do you say these in your language?

over there

Her hair's fair.

really

near the door

Go on.

Excuse me.

Would you like to dance?

Stupid!

The answer is 'No'.

All right?

It's very funny.

6 Work in a group of four. Each person takes a part. Read the story.

FOLLOW UP

7 Complete this conversation.

Vince Where's .... girlfriend, Terry?

Terry What girlfriend?

Vince Your date — the .... with

blond .... I .... see her.

Terry She's .... there .... the door.

Vince She hasn't .... blond hair. But

why .... you with her?

Terry .... you see .... big guy with her?

Vince Yes, I ....

Terry That's her ....

Vince Oh.

29

LANGUAGE WORK

can / can't

BUILD UP

1 Put these words in the table.

can't dance hear We can They

I		
He		
She	....	see.
It		....
....	....	....
You		
....		

Note: 'can't' is the short form of 'cannot'.

Questions with can/can't

2 a Look at the Victoria Road story. Complete these sentences:

.... that girl over there?

.... hear?

b Use the words in the table in Exercise 1. Put them in this table.

	....	
....	....	...............?
....	....	...............?
	....	...............?
	....	
	....	

3 a Ask people in your class what they can do.

Example
A 'Can you speak English?'
B 'Yes, I can.'

Use these cues.

speak English

swim

play the guitar

read music

play badminton

dance

sing

ski

drive a car

b Tell the class what you find out.

Example
He can play tennis. He can swim. He can't play the guitar. He can't read music.

FOLLOW UP

4 Look at the pictures in Exercise 3. Can you do these things? Write your answers.

READING

1 🔊 **Listen and repeat.**

Sunday   Monday   Tuesday   Wednesday   Thursday   Friday   Saturday

2 **Here's Terry's school timetable. Read Terry's homework diary and complete the timetable.**

	MONDAY	TUESDAY	WEDNESDAY	THURSDAY	FRIDAY
9.00			R E G I S T R A T I O N		
9.10			A S S E M B L Y		
9.30	English	Technology	Technology	Geography	Science
10.25	*Mrs Jones*				
10.40			B R E A K		
	R.E. *Snoozing*	. . . .	*boring* History	. . . .	English
11.35					
	French	Maths	. . . .	Technology	Maths
12.30					
1.25			L U N C H		
1.30			R E G I S T R A T I O N		
	. . . .	♪ ♫	Science	French	. . . .
2.25					
	Maths	English	Science	*physical exhaustion* P.E.	Art
3.20					

Homework diary

Monday
English: pp 16-17 ex 6 and 7 for Wed. ✓
French: learn new words p 62 for ✓
  test on Tues.

Tuesday
Tech: computers p 17 ex 9 for Fri.
Maths: p 18 for Thurs.
Music: practise song p 23 for next Tues.

Wednesday
Science: write report on experiment
  for Mon.

3 **Compare Terry's school timetable to yours.**

a **Make a chart like this.**

Terry's school	our school

b **Complete the chart with this information.**

How many subjects has Terry got? What are they?
How many subjects have you got? What are they?
How many periods has Terry got of each subject?
How many periods have you got of each subject?

c **What differences are there? What things are the same?**

4 **Ask people in your class: 'What are your two favourite subjects?'**

A GAME

5 **Look at Terry's timetable for one minute.**

A Close your book.
B Ask questions.

Example
B 'Has Terry got French on Monday?'
A 'Yes, he has.'
B 'You're right.' (or 'You're wrong.')

FOLLOW UP

6 Write your timetable in English.

LISTENING

Telling the time

1 Look at the photos of the clocks.

a **What do you think the missing times are?**

b **Listen and complete the times.**

c **Listen again and repeat.**

five past two   .... to five

eight o'clock   half past four   .... to ten   ten .... eleven   twenty to three

quarter past one   twenty .... nine   ten to twelve   twenty-five past seven   ....

2 **Listen and put the hands on the clocks.**

....

....

....

3 Work with a partner. Look at the clocks in Exercise 2. Ask and answer.

A Point to a clock face and ask, 'What's the time?'.
B Give the answer.

FOLLOW UP

4 Write the times under the clocks in Exercise 2.

INTERACTION

Kamala's appointment

1 Kamala is making an appointment at the dentist.

a Put the conversation in the correct order.

☐ Yes, can you come at 10.30?

☐ Thank you, Kamala.

☐ No, I'm sorry, not on Wednesday. Can you come on Thursday at 5.15?

☐ Thank you. Bye.

☐ Can I have an appointment for next Wednesday, please?

☐ Goodbye.

☐ It's Kamala Wijeratne.

☐ Quarter past five? Yes, that's OK.

☐ No, I can't come in the morning. Have you got an appointment in the afternoon after 4 o'clock?

☐ Fine. So that's 5.15 next Thursday. And what is your name?

b Listen and check your answer.

on / at

BUILD UP

2 **a** Complete this sentence.

Can you come .... Thursday .... 5.15?

b Complete this rule.

> We use .... with days and .... with times.

3 Write the correct preposition.

.... Saturday	.... quarter past ten
.... five o'clock	.... 7.42
.... Wednesday	.... five to three
.... Tuesday	.... Friday
.... Sunday	.... 9.15

4 Work with a partner. Act the dialogue from Exercise 1.

5 **a** Work with a partner. Make new dialogues.

A Ask for an appointment.
B Give a day and time.
A You can't go at that time (or on that day). Ask for another time (or day).
B Give a new time (or day).
A Accept.
B Ask for the person's name.

b Exchange roles and make a new dialogue.

FOLLOW UP

6 Write one of your dialogues from Exercise 5.

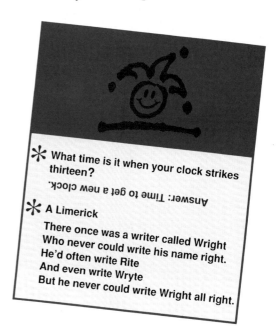

✳ What time is it when your clock strikes thirteen?

Answer: Time to get a new clock.

✳ A Limerick

There once was a writer called Wright
Who never could write his name right.
He'd often write Rite
And even write Wryte
But he never could write Wright all right.

PROJECT

My ideal school timetable

What do you think of your school timetable?

- Do you like your lessons?
- What lessons would you really like to have at school?

  Example

  pop music, sport, karate, driving

- When would you really like to be at school?
- Would you like to start earlier or later?
- Would you like to have a shorter day?
- Would you like to go to school on Sundays, too?

Write your ideal school timetable. Show the subjects and the times of your lessons.

Learning diary

A Look at the first page of this unit. How well do you know these things now? Look at each point in the contents list.

4

If you know it well, draw a happy face.

If you know it fairly well, draw a face like this.

If you don't know it well, draw a sad face.

B Try the self-check in the Workbook.

C Compare your answers with a partner. Discuss any problems with your teacher.

▶ Pronunciation: page 112

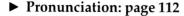

Contents

The main grammar points in this unit are:

imperatives

there is / are

There is a computer on the table.
There are two books on the table.
There isn't a bag on the table.
Is there a pen on the table?

At the cafe

1 Look at the story.
- Who are the people?
- What do you know about them?
- Where are they?
- Why is Terry angry with Sue?

2 📼 Listen and follow in your book.

Kamala It's half past four. I must go, Sue.

Sue Oh, don't go, Kam. Here's Terry. He's still angry with me.

Kamala I'm sorry, Sue. I've got an appointment at the dentist and I mustn't be late.

Sue Oh, OK. See you tomorrow.

Kamala Hi, Terry.

Sue Hi, Terry.

Terry Hello, Kamala.

Terry A cheeseburger and a chocolate milk shake, please.

Assistant That's £1.75, please.

Sue Sit here, Terry.

Terry Don't talk to me, Sue. I'm not friends with you.

Sue Don't be silly, Terry. Put your tray here.

Terry Don't touch it!

Sue Be careful, Terry!

Terry Oh, my drink!

Darren Aargh. You again!

Terry Get out of the way!

Darren Come here!

VICTORIA ROAD

 3

Right, Wrong or Don't know?

	✓	✗	?
a Sue and Kamala are at the cafe.	❏	❏	❏
b Sue has got an appointment at the dentist.	❏	❏	❏
c Kamala's appointment is at five o'clock.	❏	❏	❏
d The dentist is near the cafe.	❏	❏	❏
e Terry isn't friends with Sue.	❏	❏	❏
f Sue's drink is a chocolate milk shake	❏	❏	❏
g Terry can't find a seat.	❏	❏	❏
h The boy is Jane Fox's boyfriend.	❏	❏	❏

4 Listen again and repeat.

Useful expressions

 5 How do you say these in your own language?

I must go.

I mustn't be late.

He's angry with me.

I'm not friends with you.

Don't be silly.

Be careful!

Get out of the way!

Come here!

Imperatives

BUILD UP

6 a Look.

Be careful!	Don't be silly!
Sit here!	Don't talk to me!
....	....
....	....

b Find more examples of imperatives in the Victoria Road story. Put them in the correct column.

c 📼 Listen and follow the instructions.

7 Work in a group of three. One person is Terry, one person is Sue, one person is all the other parts. Read the story.

FOLLOW UP

8 Answer these questions in full sentences.

a Where are Kamala and Sue?
b What's the time?
c Why must Kamala go?
d What is Terry's drink?
e How much are Terry's cheeseburger and drink?
f Who is the boy at the next table?

READING

A computer

1 Look at the pictures on the envelope.

- What are they about?
- Look at the monitor. Read the instructions on the screen.
- Find the name of this:

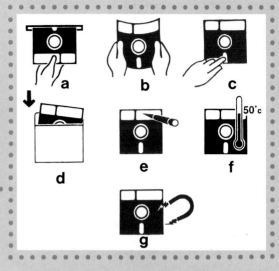

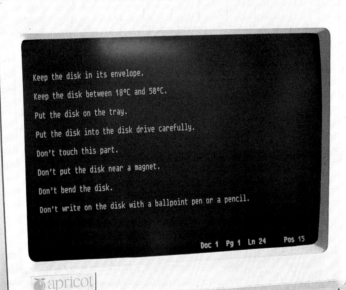

Keep the disk in its envelope.

Keep the disk between 18°C and 50°C.

Put the disk on the tray.

Put the disk into the disk drive carefully.

Don't touch this part.

Don't put the disk near a magnet.

Don't bend the disk.

Don't write on the disk with a ballpoint pen or a pencil.

Doc 1   Pg 1   Ln 24   Pos 15

2 **a** Match the instructions on the screen to the correct picture. Note there are eight instructions but only seven pictures.

b One of the instructions is not a real instruction. Which one?

3 How did you match the instructions and the pictures? What clues did you use?

4 Label these things in the pictures.

an envelope	a ballpoint pen
a magnet	a disk
a monitor	a keyboard
a disk drive	a screen

must / mustn't

5 a Look at the Victoria Road story. Complete these.

I .... go.

I .... be late.

b Translate the sentences.

6 Say what you must and mustn't do with a computer disk.

Example
You must put the disk into the disk drive carefully.

FOLLOW UP

7 Write five things that you must do and five things that you mustn't do in your classroom.

INTERNATIONAL WORDS

A lot of computer words are international. Look at the computer words on this page. Are they the same in your language?

Here are some more words. Do you know what they are?

a bit   a kilobyte

a mouse

a VDU (Visual Display Unit)

a floppy disk

hardware   software   RAM

ROM   a hard disk

A lot of other words are the same or very similar in different languages.

Do you recognize any of these words? What are they in your language?

a supermarket	sport
a disco	a hi-fi
a bar	a stereo
a toilet	a video
a shop	jeans
a sandwich	coffee
a jumbo jet	a menu
a pizza	a restaurant
a film	football
pop music	a goal

Find some more words in this book that are the same or similar in your language.

What words has your language given to English?

House for sale

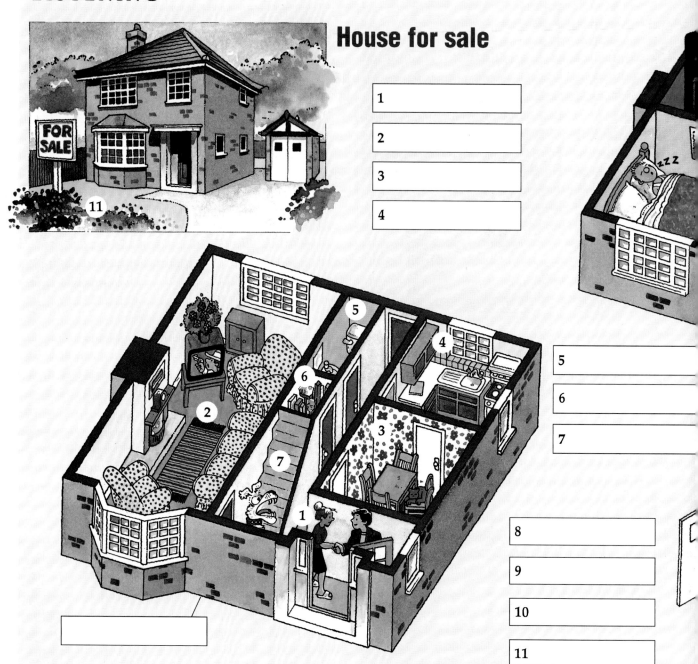

1	
2	
3	
4	

5	
6	
7	

8	
9	
10	
11	

 1

a 🛏 **Look at this house. Some people want to buy it. Listen and match these words to the correct places.**

dining room	hall	toilet
upstairs	stairs	cupboard
living room	garage	kitchen
downstairs	bedroom	
bathroom	garden	

b **Label the diagram.**

c **Listen again. Find another word for 'toilet'.**

there is / there are

BUILD UP

2 **Complete the table with these words.**

isn't   are   is

	....	a cellar.
There	....	
	....	three bedrooms.

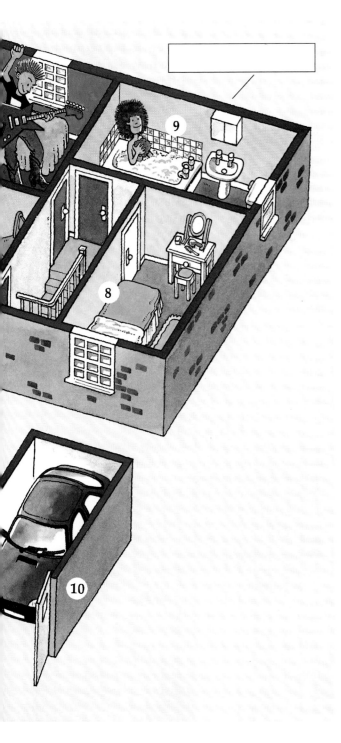

BUILD UP

4 a **Complete the questions.**

There is a garage.

.... a garage?

There are two toilets.

.... two toilets?

b **How do we make questions with 'there is / are'? Explain in your own language.**

5 a **Work with a partner. One person is the buyer. One is the seller of the house. Ask and answer.**

Example
A *How many rooms are there upstairs?*
B *There are four rooms upstairs.*
A *Is there a garage?*
B *Yes, there is.*

Use these cues.

How many rooms / upstairs?
a garage?
a cellar?
two gardens?
How many bedrooms?
a toilet / downstairs?
How many rooms / downstairs?

b **Ask your partner about his / her house or flat.**

Example
How many rooms are there in your house?

FOLLOW UP

6 a **Learn the new words.**

b **Write your dialogues from Exercise 5a.**

3 **Look at the house again. Complete these sentences with the correct word.**

a There .... two toilets.

b There .... a loo under the stairs.

c There .... a cellar.

d There .... two bathrooms.

e There .... two gardens.

f There .... a bathroom downstairs.

g There .... eight rooms in the house.

h There .... three bedrooms.

i There .... a cupboard downstairs.

✳ How can you tell if an elephant has been in the fridge?

Answer: Because there are footprints in the butter.

41

INTERACTION

Polite requests

1 Look at these requests and answers.

a Match the requests to the answers.

Excuse me. Would you like to dance?
Excuse me. Where's the loo?
Excuse me. What's the time?
Excuse me. Have you got change
    for a pound?
Excuse me. Is there a telephone
    near here?
Excuse me. Can you speak English?
Excuse me. What's that called in English?

It's five past nine.
It's a tree.
Yes, here you are.
Yes, please.
Yes, I can. Can I
    help you?
Yes, there's one in
    King Street.
It's upstairs.

b Match your dialogues to the correct pictures.

c Work with a partner. Practise the dialogues.

2 Here are some different answers to the requests. Make new dialogues with these answers.

No, I'm sorry. I can't.
I'm sorry. I don't know.
No, I'm sorry. I haven't.

3 Work with a partner.

A Make a request.
B Give an answer.

FOLLOW UP

4 Write your dialogues from Exercise 1b.

42

PROJECT

My home

Draw a plan of your home and label the rooms.

Write about your home.

- Is it a house or a flat?
- Where is it?
- How many rooms are there?
- Is there a balcony, a garden or a cellar?

Do you like your home? Say what you like or don't like. Say why.

Look at the places on this page. Would you like to live in any of them? Say why.

Learning diary

A Look at the first page of this unit. How well do you know these things now? Look at each point in the contents list.

If you know it well, draw a happy face.

If you know it fairly well, draw a face like this.

If you don't know it well, draw a sad face.

B Try the self-check in the Workbook.

C Compare your answers with a partner. Discuss any problems with your teacher.

5

6 revision

READING

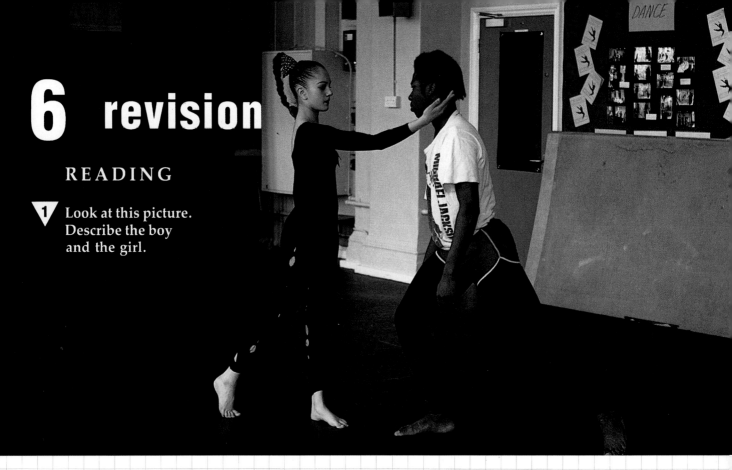

1 Look at this picture. Describe the boy and the girl.

2 Read this text about the boy.

Justin Gleeson is a dancer. He's 16 and he's a student at the Liverpool School of Music and Dance. He isn't from Liverpool. His home is in London.

The students have dance lessons in the afternoon. But in the morning they must do other school subjects. Justin's favourite subjects are Science, French and Music. He can't sing, but he can play the guitar.

Justin has got a brother and a sister. But he is the only dancer in the family. His brother is an engineer and his sister is a doctor. His parents are both teachers.

3 Complete this interview with Justin.

Interviewer Hello. Today I'm at the Liverpool

School .... Here's one of

the students. .... ?

Justin Justin Gleeson.

Interviewer .... 'Gleeson'?

Justin G – L – double E – S – O – N.

Interviewer ...., Justin?

Justin I'm 16.

Interviewer .... Liverpool?

Justin No, I'm not. I'm from London.

Interviewer Tell me about the school.

Justin We have dance lessons ....

................................., but in the morning

.... other school subjects.

Interviewer What ....

.... ?

Justin Science, French and Music.

Interviewer .... ?

Justin No, I can't, but .... the guitar.

Interviewer Are you the only dancer in your family?

Justin Yes, I am. My brother is ....

and .... doctor.

Interviewer And your .... ?

Justin My mum and dad ....

4 Work with a partner. Role play the dialogue.

5 Your partner is a student at the School of Music and Dance. He / She can be a dancer, a singer or a musician. Interview him / her.

FOLLOW UP

6 Write your interview from Exercise 5.

LANGUAGE WORK

1 a 📼 Listen and complete the clock faces. Write the times under the clocks.

1 ....

4 ....

2 ....

5 ....

3 ....

6 ....

b Work with a partner. Use your completed clocks. Ask and answer.

A 'What's the time?'

B 'It's ....'

2 Match the questions and answers to make dialogues.

Would you like to dance?
It's quarter to nine.
How much are these pens?
Can you swim?
Would you like a drink?
It's over there.
How much is this badge?
No, thank you. I've got a milk shake.
No, I can't.
What's the time?
They're 60p each.
Yes, please.
It's 85p.
Where's the loo?

3 Write down the names of:

6 rooms
4 sports
3 kinds of clothes
3 drinks
6 members of a family
5 colours
6 school subjects
5 things in a classroom
4 days of the week

4 Look at these pictures.

a Complete this description of the first girl.

She .... got .... hair and brown ....

Her .... is short.

b Describe the other people.

FOLLOW UP

5 Add one more word to each list in Exercise 3.

45

☆STAR SQUARE☆

Don't be a square. Try the Star Square.
Find the names of these singers and groups in the square.

- Duran Duran
- Wham
- Elton John
- the Beatles
- Simple Minds
- Madonna
- New Kids on the Block
- Status Quo
- Depeche Mode
- Genesis
- Black Box
- ZZ Top

- Roxy Music
- Wet Wet Wet
- Eric Clapton
- Dire Straits
- Queen
- AC DC
- Neil Young
- Vanilla Ice
- Aha
- Abba
- the Police
- the Rolling Stones

```
P O T H E B A L M C L A P T J M C C
T N E W K I D S O N T H E B L O C K
L H J M A D O N N A B A W K I D L I
T H E R O L L I N G S T O N E S E D
K I B B N N S I M P H Z Z T K S L G
D T L U E N T D I R E S T R A I T S
W H A M I A A E P O N R H G P M O T
Z N C O L N T O W E E O E A E P N O
Z N K L Y J U L E N F X P D R L J N
T E B D O O S U E Y O Y O U I E O E
O S O S U H Q T L S B M L S C M H A
P I X N N P U C R B E U I P C I N T
A C D C G E O M A H U S C N L N H A
V A N I L L A I C E E I E E A D Q C
W E T W E T W E T N U C A W P S U D
K A B B V A P L E U R A B K T P E G
A I T S L E N G W H O M B I O T S M
M S D Y D U R A N D U R A N N L I N
```

POP CHAIN

STONE COLD LOVE ME BABY I LOVE YOU BELONG TO ME AND MY GIRL IN MY DREAMS OF YOU CAN DO IT MUST BE LOVE ME OR LEAVE ME AND YOU ARE THE ONE WAY TICKET TO RIDE THE LOVE TRAIN TO YOUR HEART OF STONE

Look at the words in the chain. There are eighteen pop song titles.

Here are the first four:

Stone Cold
Cold Love
Love Me, Baby
Baby, I Love You

Find the other fourteen.

Answers

Stone Cold
Cold Love
Love Me, Baby
Baby I Love You
Love Me, Baby
You Belong To Me
Me And My Girl
Girl In My Dreams
Dreams Of You
You Can Do It

It Must Be Love
Love Me Or Leave Me
Me And You
You Are The One
One Way Ticket
Ticket To Ride
Ride The Love Train
Train To Your Heart
Heart Of Stone

► Pronunciation: page 112

46

7 sport

Contents

The main grammar point in this unit is:

the present simple tense

I live in Victoria Road.

Sue lives in Victoria Road too.

I don't live in Victoria Road.

She doesn't live in Victoria Road.

They don't live in Victoria Road.

Where do you live?

Does Vince live in Victoria Road?

Do you know Terry Moore?

1 Look at the story.

- Who are the people?
- Where are they?
- What are they talking about? Why?

He lives in Victoria Road at number 20.

Where does he live?

Excuse me. Do you know Terry Moore?

Oh yes, I know Terry.

Are you his friend?

Oh, yes. Terry knows me

Casey We come home at half past three.

Darren Does Terry come home at half past three every day?

Casey Er, no. On Wednesday he plays table tennis after school. He comes home late.

Darren On Wednesday? Hmm. What time does he come home?

Casey He gets the quarter past four bus, I think.

Darren Thank you. That's very helpful.

Casey That's OK. I must tell Terry about you.

Darren Oh no, don't do that. It's a surprise.

Casey Oh, I see. OK.

Why does Darren Tooley want Terry? What is the surprise?

2 Listen and follow in your books.

Darren Excuse me. Do you know Terry Moore?

Casey Oh yes, I know Terry. Are you his friend?

Darren What? . . . Oh, yes. Terry knows me. Where does he live?

Casey He lives in Victoria Road at number 20.

Darren What time does he go to school?

Casey He goes to school with me and some other friends. We get the bus at 8.15.

Darren When do you come home?

3 Answer these questions.

a Who does Darren Tooley want?
b Where does Terry live?
c When does Terry go to school?
d Who does he go with?
e How do they go to school?
f What time do they come home?
g What does Terry do on Wednesday?
h What time does he come home on Wednesday?
i Why mustn't Casey tell Terry about the boys?

4 Listen to the story again and repeat.

VICTORIA ROAD   48

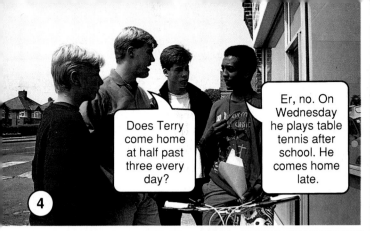

b Complete this table with 'lives' and 'live'.

I You We They	....	in Victoria Road.
		at number 20.
He She It	....	here.

Useful expressions

5 How do you say these in your language?

We get the bus.

He comes home late.

the quarter past four bus

That's very helpful.

Don't do that.

It's a surprise.

Oh, I see.

c When do we add -s to the verb?

Complete the rule.

> **We add 's' with ...., ... and it.**

7 Work with a partner. One person is Darren Tooley and one is Casey. Read the dialogue.

FOLLOW UP

8 Complete these sentences about Terry with the correct verb. Then write a sentence about your own life.

a Terry .... in Victoria Road.

I ....

b Terry .... to school with his friends.

I ....

c Terry .... the bus to school.

I ....

d Terry .... home at half past three.

I ....

e Terry .... table tennis.

I ....

The present simple tense

BUILD UP

6 a Look at the Victoria Road story. Complete these sentences.

I .... Terry.

Terry .... me.

We .... home at half past three.

He .... home late.

This is the present simple tense. It describes regular activities.

49

READING

A ftballer's week

1 Look at these pictures. What are they about?

1 ————— 5 —————

2 ————— 6 —————

3 ————— 7 —————

4 ————— 8 —————

2 Read the text. Write the day below each picture.

Every Saturday afternoon Bobby Best plays football. He is the goalkeeper for Barchester United. What does he do for the rest of the week?

'Sunday and Monday are my weekend. On Sunday I go out with my girlfriend. On Monday my girlfriend goes to work. She works in a bank. I get up late and then I play golf in the afternoon.

From Tuesday to Friday I go to the club at 9 o'clock. The team practises in the morning. On Tuesday the team doctor sees all the players. On Wednesday the manager shows a video of Saturday's match. When we practise on Thursday, the manager watches all the players. In the afternoon he chooses the new team.

On Saturday I get up at 9.30, and I have breakfast. I go to the club at 1 o'clock and the match starts at 2.30.'

3 📷 Listen. You will hear the footballer talking about his week. What do you notice about these words?

practises   watches   chooses

4 Use the pictures. Describe Bobby Best's week.

Example
He plays football on Saturday afternoon.

5 Find examples of these things in the pictures. Label them.

team   doctor   player   match
manager   goalkeeper   football club

6 Answer these questions.

a Do you like football?
b What is your favourite team?
c Who is the manager?
d Who is your favourite player?
e When do football clubs play matches in your country?

FOLLOW UP

7 Write the answers to Exercise 4.

LISTENING

Karen's day

 1 **Look at the picture. Listen and find this information.**

a What is the girl's name?
b What does she want to be?
c Where does she live?
d What is unusual about her day?

2 a **Look at the chart.**

activity	time
get up	
go to the skating rink	
practise	
have a shower	
get dressed	
go to school	
come home	
have tea	
do her homework	
go to bed	

b **Listen again. Write the times in the chart.**

The present simple tense: negative

BUILD UP

 3 a **Look at these sentences about Karen.**

She **doesn't go** to the cinema.
She **goes** to bed.

I **don't practise** on Sundays.
I **practise** every day from Monday to Saturday.

b **Complete this table with 'don't' and 'doesn't'.**

I		go to school.
You	....	live in Victoria Road.
We		
They		get up at 4 o'clock.
He		
She	....	play the guitar.
It		

c **Is there an -s ending after 'doesn't'?**

4 ▼ Does Karen do these things? Complete the sentences.

Example
She gets up at four o'clock.
She doesn't catch the bus to the skating rink.

a She ....at four o'clock. (get up)

b She .... the bus to the rink. (catch)

c She .... in the afternoon. (practise)

d Mrs Spencer .... Karen to the skating rink. (take)

e Karen .... for three hours a day. (practise)

f Karen .... to the cinema in the evening. (go)

g She .... to be a dancer. (want)

h She .... school at four o'clock. (finish)

i She .... in bed on Sundays. (stay)

j She .... to bed at 7.15. (go)

5 ▼ What does Karen say?

Example
I get up at four o'clock.
I don't catch the bus to the rink.

6 ▼ What do you think about Karen's life?

FOLLOW UP

7 ▼ Use your chart from Exercise 2a. Describe Karen's day. Start like this.

Karen gets up at four o'clock in the morning.

INTERACTION

The present simple tense: questions

BUILD UP

1 ▼ a Look at the Victoria Road story on page 48. Complete these questions.

.... know Terry Moore?
What time .... go to school?

b **Find more examples of questions in the story.**

c **Complete this table with these words.**

you I she Do they he we it Does

	....	live in Victoria Road?
....	....	play tennis?
	....	like American football?
....	....	get the bus to school?
	....	

d **Look at these sentences. What happens to the -s ending?**

She lives here.
Does she live here?

He gets the bus.
Does he get the bus?

e **Complete these sentences.**

Terry plays table tennis.

Does Terry .... table tennis?

Kamala watches TV.

Does Kamala .... TV?

a Look at the text about the footballer's week on page 50. Here is part of an interview with him. Complete the questions. Use the verbs in brackets.

Interviewer Do you go to work on Sunday and Monday?

Footballer No, I don't. That's my weekend.

Interviewer What .... on Sunday? (do)

Footballer I go out with my girlfriend.

Interviewer .... your girlfriend on Monday, too? (see)

Footballer No, I don't. She goes to work.

Interviewer Where ....? (work)

Footballer In a bank.

Interviewer What .... on Monday? (do)

Footballer I get up late and then I play golf in the afternoon.

Interviewer When .... to the club? (go)

Footballer I go to the club at 9 o'clock from Tuesday to Friday.

Interviewer When ....
.... ? (practise)

Footballer Every morning.

Interviewer When ....
the players? (see)

Footballer On Tuesday.

b Make three more questions and answers for the footballer.

c Work with a partner. Act your interview.

AN INTERVIEW

 a Choose a sports star.

b Make six questions to ask the sports star. Use:

How? What? When? Where? Do? Why?

c Act your interview with a partner.

FOLLOW UP

 Write your interview with the sports star in Exercise 3.

PERSONAL FACT FILE
A DAY IN YOUR LIFE

What is your life like?
Answer these twenty questions.

a What time do you get up?

b What's the first thing that you do when you get out of bed?

c What do you have for breakfast?

d When do you leave for school?

e How do you get to school?

f What's your favourite subject? Why?

g Who do you sit with at school?

h Who would you like to sit with?

i When do you go home?

j Do you go home at the same time every day?

k What's the first thing that you do when you get home?

l How much homework do you get each day?

m How long do you watch television each day?

n What are your favourite programmes?

o How often do you go out with your friends?

p Where do you go?

q What do you want to do when you grow up?

r What do you want for your next birthday?

s What time do you go to bed?

t What's the last thing that you do before you get into bed?

PROJECT

A sports survey

Conduct a sports survey in your class.

a Make a questionnaire. Use the questionnaire opposite to help you.

b Use your questionnaire. Interview people in your class.

c Make graphs to show your results. Write about your results. The graphs below will help you.

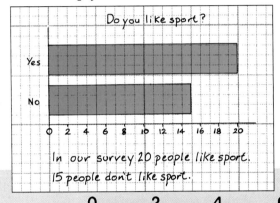

Do you like sport?

Yes

No

0 2 4 6 8 10 12 14 16 18 20

In our survey 20 people like sport.
15 people don't like sport.

SPORTS   QUESTIONNAIRE

Name ....

Address ....
....
....

*Do you like sport? Yes ☐ No ☐

*Do you play a sport in your free time?
Yes ☐ No ☐

What do you play? ....
....

*Do you watch sport on TV? Yes ☐ No ☐

*Do you go to sports events? Yes ☐ No ☐

*please put a tick in the appropriate box

0 2 4 6 8 10 12 14 16

0 2 4 6 8

What sports do you play?

Twelve people in our class play football.

Fifteen people in our class play . . . .

Learning diary

7

A Look at the first page of this unit. How well do you know these things now? Look at each point in the contents list.

If you know it well, draw a happy face.

If you know it fairly well, draw a face like this.

If you don't know it well, draw a sad face.

B Try the self-check in the Workbook.

C Compare your answers with a partner. Discuss any problems with your teacher.

▶ Pronunciation: page 113

54

8 time out

Contents
Grammar points

The main grammar point in this unit is:

some / any

HAVE YOU GOT ANY MONEY?

Kamala misses the bus

1 Look at the story.

- Who are the people?
- Where are they?
- What is happening?
- Why does Sue give her bags to Kamala?
- What happens to Kamala?

OK. Here you are. Give them to Vince, if you see him or my mum if you see her.

Come on, Sue. I don't want to miss the bus.

Hey, Kam. Can you take my coat and bags with you?

There's a good film at the cinema this week.

Let's go after school.

OK. What about you, Kam?

I can't. I help in the shop after school.

Kamala Come on, Sue. I don't want to miss the bus.

Sue OK. Here you are. Give them to Vince, if you see him or my mum if you see her. Thanks, Kam. Bye.

Kamala Blimey, Sue. These bags are heavy. Oh no. There's the bus.

Kamala Stop. Wait. Oh, damn!

2 🎧 Listen and follow in your book.

Girl 1 There's a good film at the cinema this week.

Girl 2 Let's go after school. Do you two want to join us?

Sue OK. What about you, Kam?

Kamala I can't. I help in the shop after school. Anyway, you do your community work at the hospital on Wednesday, Sue.

Sue Oh, it's all right. I can go on Saturday.
Later

Sue Hey, Kam. Can you take my coat and bags with you? I don't want to take them to the cinema.

Kamala Oh, all right, but I can't take them to your house. I'm in a hurry.

Sue It doesn't matter. There's nobody at home. Mum has got a driving lesson and Vince plays football on Wednesday.

3 Right, Wrong or Don't know?

		✓	✗	?
a	It's Monday.	☐	☐	☐
b	Sue goes to the cinema after school every Wednesday.	☐	☐	☐
c	Kamala wants to go to the cinema.	☐	☐	☐
d	Kamala goes to dance classes after school.	☐	☐	☐
e	Kamala doesn't want to take Sue's coat and bags.	☐	☐	☐
f	Sue works at the hospital on Wednesday.	☐	☐	☐
g	Sue's mother is at work.	☐	☐	☐
h	Mr Scott comes home at six o'clock.	☐	☐	☐
i	Vince plays football with Casey.	☐	☐	☐
j	Kamala's bags are very heavy.	☐	☐	☐
k	Kamala misses the bus.	☐	☐	☐

Blimey, Sue. These bags are heavy.

Oh no. There's the bus.

Stop. Wait. Oh, damn!

4 Listen again and repeat.

Useful expressions

5 How do you say these in your language?

Let's ....

you two

What about you?

It's all right.

I'm in a hurry.

It doesn't matter.

There's nobody at home.

There's the bus.

Oh, damn!

Object pronouns

BUILD UP

6 a Look.

I LOVE HER. SHE LOVES ME.

| I | love | her. |
| She | loves | me. |

This is a subject pronoun.   **This is an object pronoun.**

b Find the other object pronouns in the Victoria Road story. Complete this list.

subject	object		subject	object
I	....		we	....
he	....		you	....
she	....		they	....
it	it			

7 Work with a partner. One person is Sue and one of the other girls, and one person is Kamala and the second girl. Read the dialogue.

FOLLOW UP

8 Answer these questions.

a What do the girls want to do after school?
b Why can't Kamala go to the cinema with the other girls?
c What does Sue do on Wednesday?
d Why doesn't Sue want to keep her coat and bags?
e Why can't Kamala take them to Sue's house?
f What does Vince do on Wednesday?
g Why isn't Sue's mother at home?
h Why is Kamala angry?

READING

1 **Read the information about Paradise Island. Label these things on the map.**

beach	souvenir shop
island	tennis court
forest	swimming pool
river	sea
disco	restaurant
cinema	supermarket

Come to Paradise Island – the holiday island for young people. Paradise Island has got two beautiful beaches. You can swim in the sea or go windsurfing.

You can have a picnic in the forest. You can climb the hills. You can fish in the river.

Or you can swim in our Olympic swimming pool.

There are lots of things to do on Paradise Island. There's a tennis court.

In the evenings you can dance at Sharks Disco. There's a cinema too. We show a new film every day.

You sleep in huts in Paradise Village.

You can buy food at the supermarket or you can eat at the Blue Dolphin restaurant.

There's a souvenir shop, too, and a post office.

Come to Paradise Island for a wonderful holiday.

 2 **What can you do on Paradise Island? Ask and answer.**

Example
Can you go windsurfing?
Yes, you can. You can go windsurfing in the sea.

Use these cues.

go windsurfing	go to the cinema	go skiing
buy clothes	fish	swim
have a picnic	buy food	dance
go to a museum	send a letter	go walking
watch television	go skating	go climbing

3 **a Look.**

Let's go **to** the cinema.   We're **at** the cinema.

b Write 'to' or 'at'.

Where's Jane? She's .... the tennis court.

We have lunch .... the restaurant.

I go .... the beach every day.

There's a good film .... the cinema.

Can you buy postcards .... the shop?

Let's go .... the disco.

Can I send this letter .... Greece, please?

Come .... Paradise Island for your holiday.

 4 **You are on Paradise Island. Plan your first three days.**

	morning	afternoon	evening
Day 1			
Day 2			
Day 3			

FOLLOW UP

 5 **Here's a postcard from someone on Paradise Island. Complete it.**

Paradise Island

Dear Jane,
I'm on Paradise .... It's a ....
island for young .... There are a .... of
things to .... here. There are two beautiful
.... and a swimming .... too. You can
play tennis at the .... and you
can climb the .... or .... a picnic ..... the
forest. And in the .... there's a disco. It's
called .... a cinema, too. They
.... a new........... every day. Hope you're well.
Love, Pete

59

LISTENING
Paradise Island

1 🔊 Listen. You will hear part of a radio programme about Paradise Island. Which of these do the people mention? Tick them.

churches

horses

snakes

sharks

lions

spiders

dogs

tigers

castles

cars

swimming pool

cinema

tennis

insects

beach

bathrooms

rivers

shops

2 What do people like about Paradise Island? What don't they like? Make a chart like this. Write what people say.

+	−
Example *The beaches are very clean.*	*There isn't a lot to do.*

3 Do you agree with the people in the interviews? What do you like on your holidays?

some / any

 4 **a** Look at this dialogue.

Are there **any** animals on the island?
There aren't **any** snakes or tigers. But there are **some** big spiders.

b When do we use 'some'? When do we use 'any'? Complete this rule.

> We use .... in positive statements.
> We use .... in negative statements.
> We use .... in questions.

 5 Here are some more things from the interviews about Paradise Island. Complete them with 'some' or 'any'.

a Are there .... shops here?

b There aren't .... cars on the island.

c Have you got .... friends here?

d They've got .... souvenirs in the shop.

e There aren't .... museums.

f There are .... interesting people here.

g Are there .... sharks in the sea?

h There are .... beautiful birds on the island.

i We usually have lunch with .... people from Greece.

 6 Work with a partner. One person is the interviewer, one is a person on Paradise Island. Use the information in your chart. Make the dialogues.

Here are some questions to help you.

Do you like Paradise Island?
What do you usually do here in the morning?
Do you like the . . . ?
Are there any . . . ?
Can you . . . ?
What do you like about Paradise Island?
What don't you like about Paradise Island?

FOLLOW UP

 7 Write a postcard from someone who doesn't like the island.

INTERACTION

Making suggestions

1 Look at the Victoria Road story on page 56. Complete these sentences.

.... go to the cinema after school.

.... join us?

2 Make dialogues. Choose from A and B.

Example
A Do you want to *go to the cinema?*
(Let's *go to the cinema.*)

B *No, I can't. I haven't got any money.*

A	B
go to the cinema	No, I can't. I must go home.
go to the beach	No, I don't want to.
go to the cafe	No, I can't. I must do my homework.
watch a video	Let's have a rest first.
listen to a record	I'm sorry. I help my parents after school.
go to the shops	No, I can't. I've got an appointment at the dentist.
play football	No, I can't. I haven't got a ticket.
go swimming	No, I can't. I haven't got any money.
go to the dance	No, I want to stay here.
climb the hill	No, I want to watch the football match on TV.

 3 **A GAME**

A 'I haven't got any pens.'
B 'I've got some pens, but I haven't got any pencils.'
C 'I've got some pens and some pencils, but I haven't got any apples.'
D 'I've got some pens and some pencils and some apples, but I haven't got any . . .'

Continue.

FOLLOW UP

4 Write your dialogues for Exercise 2.

PROJECT

Holiday

**What is your ideal place for a holiday?
It can be a real or an imaginary place.**

- Draw a map of your place.
- Label the buildings and other features.
- Write a leaflet about the place. Say what you can do there.
- Illustrate your leaflet with some pictures.
- Write a postcard from there to someone you know.

KENYA

Come to Kenya for an unforgettable holiday.

Dear Carol and Peter
Kenya is great! The beaches
are beautiful. At the
moment, we're on safari.
There are lots of animals —
lions, giraffes, zebras.
Hope you're well. Bye.
love Alan and Mary

Carol and Peter Long
42 Walton Street
OXFORD
OX7 3BT
ENGLAND

Stay in one of the fine hotels on the Kenyan coast. Don't worry about the language. Everybody here speaks English. You can sunbathe on the beautiful beaches. Lie on the white sand. Swim in the warm blue water of the Indian Ocean. Or, you can spend a day on a dhow.

But don't spend all your time on the beach. This is Africa and Africa means safaris. You can go on safari to one of the national parks. Here you can see lions, elephants, giraffes, zebras, flamingoes and many other animals. And from the Amboseli national park you can see Africa's highest mountain, Mt. Kilimanjaro. Don't forget your camera!

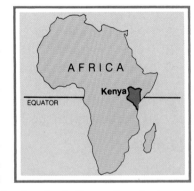

AFRICA

Kenya

EQUATOR

Learning diary

A Look at the first page of this unit. How well do you know these things now? Look at each point in the contents list.

If you know it well, draw a happy face.

If you know it fairly well, draw a face like this.

If you don't know it well, draw a sad face.

B Try the self-check in the Workbook.

C Compare your answers with a partner. Discuss any problems with your teacher.

8

► **Pronunciation: page 113**

Contents

The main grammar point in this unit is:

the present continuous tense

She's wearing jeans.
She isn't wearing a dress.
Is she wearing a blouse?

She's wearing jeans today.
But she doesn't wear jeans
when she goes to school.
She wears a school uniform.

A strange girl

1 Look at the story.

- Who are the people?
- Where are they?
- Why is Kamala carrying Sue's coat and bags?
- What are the three boys doing? Why?
- What does Terry do? Why?

Look, Terry. I must go. I'm late.

Wait a minute, Kam. Give me Sue's coat and bags.

Hi, Kam. Why are you carrying those bags and that coat?

They're Sue's. But I can't explain now.

What are you doing?

I'm hiding from those three guys round the corner.

2 🎧 Listen and follow in your books.

Terry Hi, Kam. Why are you carrying those bags and that coat?

Kamala They're Sue's. But I can't explain now. I'm in a hurry.

Kamala What's the matter, Terry? What are you doing?

Terry I'm hiding from those three guys round the corner.

Terry What are they wearing?

Kamala Well, one of them is wearing a red sweater and jeans; one is wearing a black jacket and grey trousers.

Terry Is the other guy wearing a blue sweatshirt?

Kamala Yes, he is.

Terry It's them. What are they doing?

Kamala Well, they aren't doing anything. They're sitting on a wall.

Kamala Look, Terry, I must go. I'm late.

Terry Wait a minute, Kam. Give me Sue's coat and bags. I can take them.

Terry Good, the big guy isn't looking at me. But the wind is blowing the hood.

Terry Oh no!

Darren There he is. Quick. Chase him.

Right, Wrong or Don't know?

		✓	✗	?
a	In picture 1, Terry and Kamala are arriving at Victoria Road.	❑	❑	❑
b	Kamala is carrying Sue's bags.	❑	❑	❑
c	Three boys are waiting at the bus stop.	❑	❑	❑
d	The three boys are Terry's friends.	❑	❑	❑
e	In picture 2 Terry is hiding from the three boys.	❑	❑	❑
f	The three boys are all wearing sweatshirts.	❑	❑	❑
g	One of the boys is Darren Tooley.	❑	❑	❑
h	The three boys are talking to a man.	❑	❑	❑
i	In picture 4 Terry is wearing Sue's coat.	❑	❑	❑
j	In the last picture, the three boys are chasing Terry.	❑	❑	❑

 Listen again and repeat.

Useful expressions

5 **How do you say these in your language?**

I can't explain.

What's the matter?

round the corner

It's them.

What are they doing?

I'm late.

Wait a minute.

There he is.

6 **Work with a partner. One person is Terry, one is Kamala and Darren Tooley. Read the dialogue.**

FOLLOW UP

7 **What is happening in each picture in the story?**

a **Complete the sentences.**

.... are sitting on a wall.

.... is wearing Sue's coat.

.... are chasing Terry.

.... is carrying Sue's bags and coat.

.... are arriving at Victoria Road.

.... is blowing the hood.

.... is hiding from the three boys.

.... are waiting for Terry.

.... is giving Sue's coat and bags to Terry.

b **Which picture does each sentence describe? Put a number next to each sentence.**

LANGUAGE WORK

The present continuous tense

BUILD UP

1 **a** Complete these sentences from the Victoria Road story.

I .... hiding.

One of them .... a red sweater.

They .... on a wall.

They .... anything.

The big guy .... at me.

This is the present continuous tense. It describes something that is happening at the moment.

b Complete this table.

I	am 'm am not 'm not	eating.
		sitting on a wall.
He She It	....	hiding. wearing trousers.
		carrying two bags.
We You They	....	waiting for the bus.

2 Look at the picture. What are the people doing?

3 Who is who? Work out which girl is Rebecca, which is Angela, which is Jean, which is Olivia and which is Lisa. Use these clues.

Lisa isn't wearing jeans.
Angela and Olivia haven't got bags.
Olivia isn't wearing a skirt.
Jean and Angela aren't wearing T-shirts.

Note:

She is **wearing** a coat.

She is **carrying** a coat.

The present continuous tense: questions

BUILD UP

4 **a** Make these into questions.

The other guy is wearing a blue sweatshirt

Is ....?

You are carrying those bags.

Why ....?

b Check your answers in the Victoria Road story.

c Complete this table with these words.

it   is   she   they   am   he   you   are   we   I

	....	....	
What	....	....	....	doing?
	....	....	
	....	....	
	....	....	

5 Look at the picture of the barbecue. Here are the answers to some questions. What were the questions ?

Example
Are Terry and Casey playing badminton?

a .... badminton?
No, they aren't. They're playing football.

b ....?
They're talking.

c ....?
A hamburger.

d Where ....?
On the picnic box.

e ....?
A magazine.

f .... cutting rolls?
No, he isn't. He's cooking.

g ....?
A red shirt.

A MIME GAME

6 **A** Mime an action.
B Ask what A is doing.

Example
B *'Are you cooking?'*
A *'No, I'm not.'*
B *'Are you washing a car?'*
A *'Yes, I am.'*

FOLLOW UP

7 Write your answers to Exercise 2.

* *Teacher*: Jane, name seven animals that live in Africa.
  Jane: A giraffe and six elephants.

* *Mother*: Jane! Why are you writing on your T-shirt?
  Jane: The teacher said we've got to write a project on clothes.

READING

1
a Look at the pictures. Which outfit do you like best? Why?

b Read the texts. Match them to the correct pictures and write the names of the people.

Sharon's wearing a pink jumper, a dark brown skirt, brown tights and brown shoes. Her jumper is £12.99 from 'Dorothy Perkins'. The jacket is grey with pink buttons and is £49.99 from 'Warehouse'. Sharon's also wearing a purple headband and pink gloves.

Ben's suit is by Dior. What do you call that colour? Brown? Pink? You describe it. With his suit Ben's wearing a brown and white shirt, a brown belt and brown shoes. He's carrying a black coat.

Where's **Katy** going in this outfit? She's wearing a black dress, tights and black shoes. Her earrings and bracelet are from 'The Jewel Shop'. The brooch on her dress is her grandmother's! Katy's carrying a black and silver bag.

Now what's **Colin** wearing? Is it a suit? Maybe, but it hasn't got trousers. It's got shorts. Colin is also wearing an orange shirt, a grey waistcoat and canvas shoes. Colin's outfit is by Byblos.

Is **David** a sports fan? He's wearing a white cricket sweater and black and white baseball boots, and he's holding a red baseball cap in his hand. The cricket sweater is £28 from 'Sportif' and the baseball cap is £8.50 from 'You'. David is also wearing jeans, red and grey socks and a black watch.

Liz's outfit is cheap and sporty. She's wearing a black sweatshirt with a hood (£18 from 'French Connection'), red shorts, black tights and black and red trainers. What has she got in that bag?

fashion parade

1

4

2

3

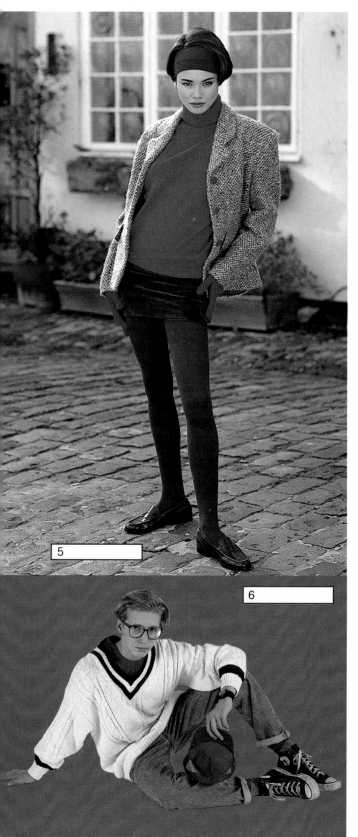

5

6

3 a Use the things in the pictures. Choose different items to make a new outfit.

  b Describe your new outfit.

4 Which outfit would you choose for these occasions?

  a You are going to a friend's birthday party.
  b You are going for a picnic.
  c You are going to the cinema.
  d You are visiting your grandparents.
  e You are helping with the housework.
  f You are going to a wedding.

W O R D   W O R K

5 How many names of clothes do you know? Put them in a chart like this. Who can make the longest list?

boys	girls	unisex

6 You are going on holiday. You can only take six things. Choose six things from your own clothes.

  Example
  My blue trousers.

FOLLOW UP

7 Describe the clothes that you are wearing now.

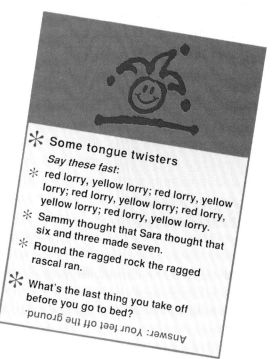

✱ Some tongue twisters
  Say these fast:
✱ red lorry, yellow lorry; red lorry, yellow lorry; red lorry, yellow lorry; red lorry, yellow lorry; red lorry, yellow lorry; red lorry, yellow lorry.
✱ Sammy thought that Sara thought that six and three made seven.
✱ Round the ragged rock the ragged rascal ran.
✱ What's the last thing you take off before you go to bed?
Answer: Your feet off the ground.

2 Find one example of each of these things in the pictures.

shirt	dress	shorts	trousers	waistcoat
belt	socks	cap	brooch	headband
suit	shoes	coat	jacket	
skirt	earrings	gloves	sweater	
tights	trainers	bag	bracelet	

A new pair of jeans

1 a Look at these pictures. Number them in the correct order to make a story.

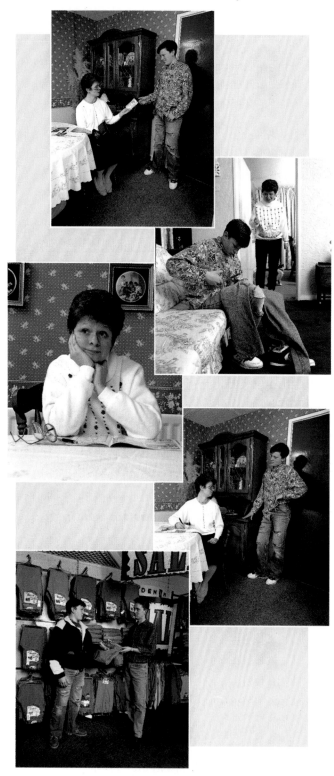

b ▄ Listen and check your order.

2 Work with a partner. Act the dialogue.

The present continuous and the present simple tense

BUILD UP

3 a Look.

A	B
Why **are you wearing** those old jeans?	People always **wear** old jeans.
I'm cutting these jeans.	People always **cut** their jeans.

b What are these two tenses?

> The present continuous tense describes what is happening now, at the moment.
> The present simple tense describes the usual situation, or what happens regularly.

4 Complete these sentences. Put the verb in brackets into the correct tense.

a We .... an English lesson at the moment. (have)

b We .... English every day. (have)

c We .... an exercise about the present continuous tense. (do)

d I .... jeans today. (wear)

e I .... jeans to school every day. (wear)

f The teacher .... at my book now. (look)

g Our teacher .... at our books every lesson. (look)

5 'Kids! I don't understand you!' Do your parents ever say this to you? What about?

FOLLOW UP

6 Complete this dialogue.

Mother Cliff! ....?

Boy .... cutting these jeans.

Mother But they're your .... jeans.

Boy People .... jeans.

.... new jeans, Mum.

Mother Kids! I .... understand you!

INTERACTION

At the clothes shop

 a Look at the pictures.

- Where are the people?
- What are they doing?

b Number the questions and answers in the correct order to make the dialogue.

- [ ] Goodbye.
- [ ] Are they all right?
- [ ] They're £18.95.
- [ ] Thank you. Goodbye.
- [ ] Yes, they're fine.
- [ ] That's £1.05 change. Thank you.
- [ ] Of course. There's a changing room over there.
- [ ] That's £18.95, then, please.
- [ ] Do you want anything else?
- [ ] How much are these jeans?
- [ ] Here you are.
- [ ] No, thank you.
- [ ] Can I try them on?

c 🔊 Listen and check your answers.

 Work with a partner. Act the dialogue.

Words with no singular

BUILD UP

 a Look.

this T-shirt   these jeans

These words are always plural.

jeans   trousers   tights   scissors

b Look at these clothes. Make dialogues.

Example
How much are these jeans?
They're £16.99.

How much is this T-shirt?
It's £7.30.

 Make shopping dialogues for these things in the pictures.

T-shirt   tracksuit   trousers   jacket

Use the dialogue in Exercise 1 to help you.

FOLLOW UP

Write your dialogues from Exercise 4 for the tracksuit and the trousers.

PROJECT

Fashion page

Make a fashion page for a magazine.

- Collect or draw pictures of clothes that you like. Or use photographs of yourself and your friends.
- Write what each model is wearing. Use the texts on page 68 to help you. There are some more useful words on this page.

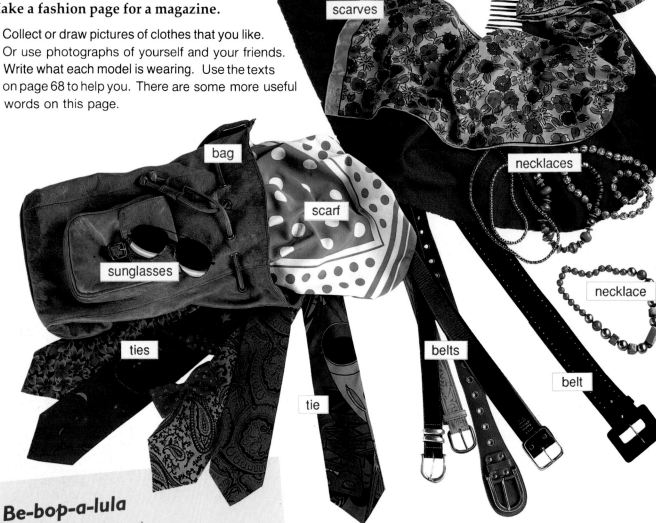

scarves

bag

scarf

necklaces

sunglasses

necklace

ties

belts

belt

tie

Be-bop-a-lula

(first recorded by Gene Vincent)

Chorus

    Be-bop-a-lula
    .... my baby.
    Be-bop-a-lula
    I .... mean maybe.
    Be-bop-a-lula
    She's .... baby.
    Be-bop-a-lula
    I don't mean maybe.
    Be-bop-a-lula
    She-e-e's my .... doll, my baby doll, my baby ....

1 See the .... with the red .... on.
   She .... do the boogie all night long.

2 See the girl in the tight, ... jeans.
   She's the .... of all the teens.

3 See the girl .... the diamond ring.
   She knows how to shake .... thing.

Learning diary

9

A Look at the first page of this unit. How well do you know these things now? Look at each point in the contents list.

If you know it well, draw a happy face.

If you know it fairly well, draw a face like this.

If you don't know it well, draw a sad face.

B Try the self-check in the Workbook.

C Compare your answers with a partner. Discuss any problems with your teacher.

▶ Pronunciation: page 113

10 revision

READING

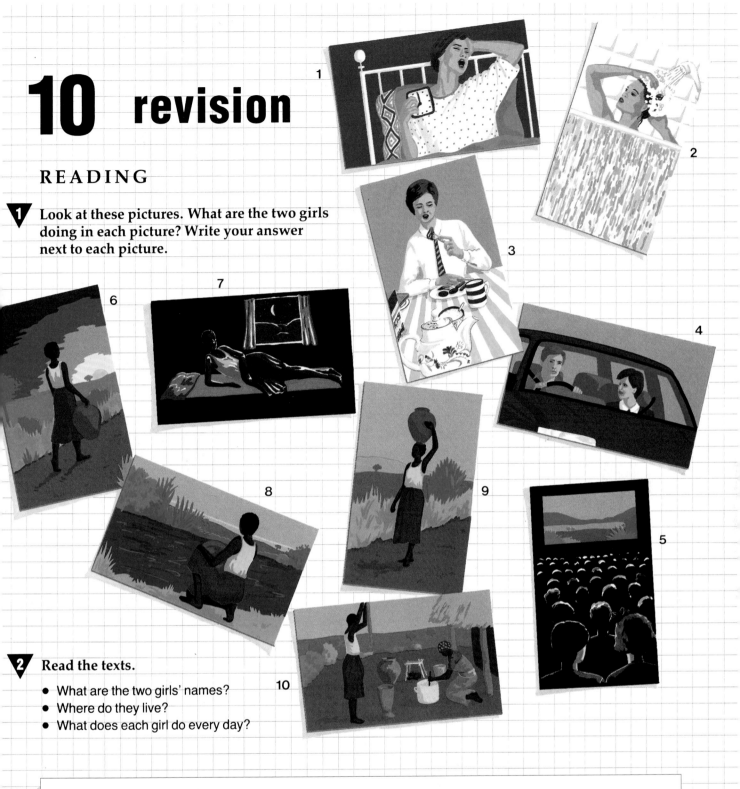

1 Look at these pictures. What are the two girls doing in each picture? Write your answer next to each picture.

2 Read the texts.

- What are the two girls' names?
- Where do they live?
- What does each girl do every day?

Selina lives in a village in Africa. Her day starts at 4 o'clock. She gets up and she walks three miles to the river. She collects some water and she carries it back to her house. It's very heavy. The water isn't clean, but there isn't any water in the village. Selina doesn't go to school. She can't read or write. She helps her mother in the house. She fetches water from the river three times every day. She goes to bed at 8 o'clock.

Kelly lives in a city in Britain. She gets up at 8 o'clock She has a shower every morning. She eats her breakfast and then she goes to school. Her father takes her to school in his car. In the evening Kelly watches television or goes to the cinema with her friends. When Kelly wants some water, she goes to the kitchen or the bathroom.

Selina and Kelly live in different worlds. But Kelly knows Selina and Selina knows Kelly. At Kelly's school there is a photograph of Selina. In Selina's village there is a photograph of Kelly's class. Why?

Selina and Kelly: Different worlds or one world?

3 Do Kelly and Selina do these things? Write sentences.

Example
Kelly goes to school.
Selina doesn't go to school.

go to school
get up at eight o'clock
live in a village
carry water
walk eighteen miles each day
travel in a car
watch television
go to the cinema

4 A local radio station is making a programme called 'One World'. An interviewer is talking to Kelly about her life and Selina's life.

a Here are Kelly's answers. What are the questions?

Interviewer ....?
Kelly I get up at eight o'clock.

Interviewer How ....?
Kelly My father usually takes me in his car.

Interviewer ....?
Kelly I watch TV or I go to the cinema with my friends.

Interviewer ....?
Kelly In a village in Africa.

Interviewer ....?
Kelly At four o'clock. And then she collects water from the river.

Interviewer Why ....?
Kelly Because there isn't any water in her village.

Interviewer ....?
Kelly No, she doesn't. She helps her mother in the house.

Interviewer ....?
Kelly At eight o'clock in the evening.

b Work with a partner. Role play the interview.

5 Why do Selina and Kelly know each other?

a Look at these pictures. What are the people doing in each picture?

b 🔊 Listen to part of the radio programme about Kelly and Selina. Put the pictures in the correct order.

6 Interview the people in the pictures. Ask them what they are doing.

Example
What are you doing?
I'm collecting bottles.

7 Do you help other people? Ask people in your class. Write what they do.

FOLLOW UP

8 Describe how Kelly and her friends help Selina.

✳ **What is a frog's favourite drink?**
Answer: Croaka Cola.

✳ **What do you get after someone has taken it?**
Answer: A photograph.

✳ **Where does Friday come before Thursday?**
Answer: In the dictionary.

LANGUAGE WORK

1 ▼ **Write down these things.**

5 sports
6 kinds of clothes
3 things that you do in the morning
3 things that you don't do in the morning
3 things that you do at the weekend
3 things that you don't do at the weekend
5 buildings
6 things that you see on a map

2 ▼ **Complete these sentences from the radio programme about Selina and Kelly. Use 'some' or 'any'.**

a There isn't .... water in the village.

b There is .... water in the river, but it isn't clean.

c There aren't .... bathrooms in the huts in the village.

d The people in the village haven't got .... money for their pipe.

e Kelly's friends send them .... money.

f Have you got .... bottles for the bottle bank?

g I've got .... cans and .... stamps.

h Has Selina got .... brothers or sisters?

GRAMMAR GAME

3 ▼ **Move round the board. When you land on a word, write it down. The first person to make a correct sentence with four or more of the words is the winner.**

FOLLOW UP

4 ▼ **Write to someone in another country.**

- Tell them about your life.
- Say how often you do things.
- Add some pictures. Say what you are doing in the pictures.

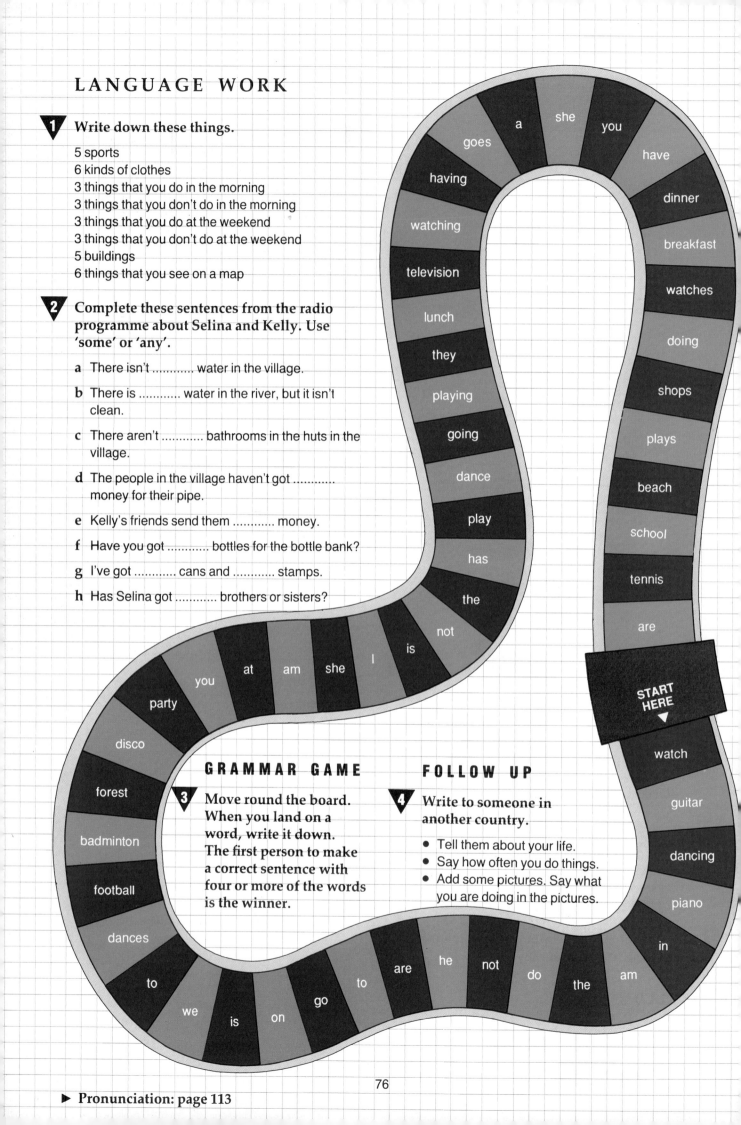

a
she
you
goes
have
having
dinner
watching
breakfast
television
watches
lunch
doing
they
shops
playing
going
plays
dance
beach
play
school
has
tennis
the
are
not
is
START HERE ▼
I
she
am
at
you
watch
party
disco
guitar
forest
badminton
dancing
football
piano
dances
in
to
he not
we
are
do
the
am
is
on
go
to

76

11 mystery

the past simple: to be / regular verbs

Contents

Grammar points

The main grammar points in this unit are:

the past simple tense: 'to be'

Yesterday in Victoria Road . . .

Sue wasn't at the hospital.
She was at the cinema.
Was Kamala at the cinema, too?

Casey and Vince weren't at the cinema.
They were in the park.
Where were Terry and Darren Tooley?

the past simple tense: regular verbs

Now	*In 1988*
Alan lives in Scotland.	*He **lived** in Scotland.*
He works in a hotel.	*He **worked** in a hotel.*

In the park

1 Look at the story.

- Who are the people?
- Where are they?
- What are they doing?
- What is in the lake?
- Why does Mrs Scott think Sue is at the hospital?

> 4-nil. You were great, Casey. Your second goal was brilliant. I...

> Hey, look at all those books on the grass near the lake.

> These are Sue's books.

> There's someone in the water. Come on.

2 🔊 Listen and follow in your books.

Vince 4-nil. You were great, Casey. Your second goal was brilliant. I thought . . .

Casey Hey, look at all those books on the grass near the lake.

Casey These are Sue's books. What are they doing here?

Vince And here's her bag under this bench.

Casey What's that over there?

Vince There's someone in the water. Come on.

Vince Oh, my God! It's Sue's coat. But where's Sue?

Casey She isn't here. Sue! Sue!

Later

Mrs Scott Now tell me again, Vince.

Vince I was in the park with Casey. We were on our way back from football.

Mrs Scott Where was Sue's coat?

Vince It was in the lake.

Mrs Scott Were the books in the water, too?

Vince No, they weren't. They were on the grass.

Mrs Scott But it's Wednesday. Sue must be at the hospital today.

Vince Well, she wasn't at the hospital half an hour ago.

Mrs Scott Oh dear! We'd better call the police.

What do you think?

- Where is Sue?
- What do Vince and Mrs Scott think?
- Why was Sue's coat in the lake?

(4) Oh, my God! It's Sue's coat. But where's Sue?

(5) Where was Sue's coat? / It was in the lake. / But it's Wednesday. Sue must be at the hospital today. / Well, she wasn't at the hospital half an hour ago.

Oh dear! We'd better call the police.

(6)

 3 Answer these questions.

1 Where were Casey and Vince?
2 Why were they there?
3 What was on the grass?
4 Where was Sue's coat?
5 Was Sue's bag in the lake?
6 Was Sue in the park?
7 Was Sue at the hospital?

 4 Listen again and repeat.

Useful expressions

 5 How do you say these in your language?

4–nil

You were great!

brilliant

What are they doing here?

Oh, my God!

on our way back from …

She must be at the hospital.

half an hour ago

Oh dear!

We'd better …

call the police

 6 Work with a partner. One person is Vince, one person is Casey and Mrs Scott. Read the dialogue.

FOLLOW UP

7 Casey is talking to his parents. Complete what he says.

.... and I were on our ....
back .... football. We were
.... the park. .... were
some books on the .... near the
.... They were .... books.
Her bag was .... a bench and her
.... was .... the water. But
Sue wasn't .... She usually does her
community work .... the hospital on
.... But .... wasn't there
today.

79

LANGUAGE WORK

The verb 'to be': past tense

BUILD UP

 a **Complete these sentences from the Victoria Road story.**

I .... in the park with Casey.

It .... in the lake.

She .... at the hospital half an hour ago.

You .... great, Casey.

We .... on our way back from football.

They .... on the grass.

No, they ....

This is the past tense of 'to be'.

b **Complete this table. Use these words.**

were   weren't   was

I He She It	.... wasn't	in the park.
		great.
We You They	....	at the hospital.

 A policewoman is interviewing Vince.

a **Complete their conversation with 'was', 'wasn't', 'were' or 'weren't'.**

Policewoman Where .... you?

Vince I .... in the park.

Policewoman Why .... you in the park?

Vince I .... on my way back from football.

Policewoman .... you alone?

Vince No, I .... My friend Casey .... with me.

Policewoman Where .... the bag?

Vince It .... under a bench.

Policewoman .... the books under the bench, too?

Vince No, they .... They .... on the grass.

Policewoman And where .... the coat?

Vince It .... in the lake.

Policewoman But your sister .... there. Is that right?

Vince No, she .... in the park. She .... at home and she .... at the hospital.

Policewoman .... she at school in the afternoon?

Vince Yes, she ....

b **Work with a partner. Act the conversation.**

The verb 'to be': past tense questions

BUILD UP

 a **Put these words in the correct order to make a statement and a question.**

	statement	question
on were the grass books the school Sue at was		

b **How do we make questions with the verb 'to be' in the past tense? Complete the rule.**

> To make questions in the past tense of the verb 'to be', we put .... or .... in front of the subject.

Years

BUILD UP

a **Look.**

1914 = nineteen fourteen
1885 = eighteen eighty-five

b **Say these years.**

1972   1945   1492   1801   1066

5 a Answer the questions.

A GENERAL KNOWLEDGE QUIZ

1 Who was the first man on the Moon?

a John Glenn
b Yuri Gagarin
c Neil Armstrong
d Buzz Aldrin

2 Where was the first man in space from?

a Russia
b America
c Germany
d Japan

3 Who was the 'King of Rock and Roll'?

a James Dean
b Elvis Presley
c Bob Dylan
d John Lennon

4 Where were the Beatles from?

a San Francisco
b London
c New York
d Liverpool

5 When was the First World War?

a 1914–18
b 1939–45
c 1910–1915
d 1885–1900

6 Where was Christopher Columbus from?

a Portugal
b Spain
c Italy
d Brazil

7 Who were the world football champions in 1986?

a Argentina
b West Germany
c the Netherlands
d Denmark

8 Where were the Olympics in 1988?

a Japan
b America
c Korea
d Greece

9 Who was the first president of the United States?

a John F. Kennedy
b George Washington
c Abraham Lincoln
d Ronald Reagan

10 Where was Superman from?

a Tristan
b Saturn
c the Moon
d Krypton

b 🔊 Listen and check your answers.

FOLLOW UP

6 Write the correct answers to the quiz in full.

READING

Was it Nessie?

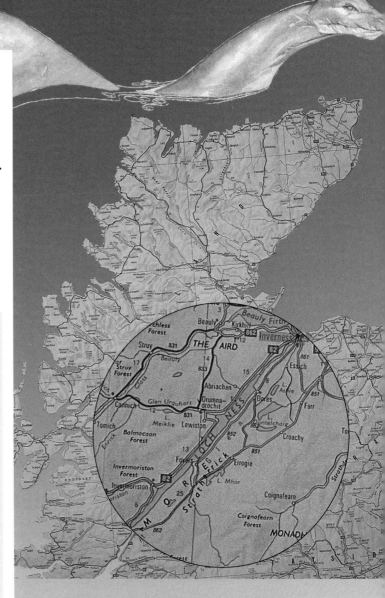

1 a Look quickly at the story and the pictures. Answer these questions.

1 What is the man's name?
2 What year was it?
3 Where was he?
4 What is the story about?

b What do you know about this topic?

My name is Alan Cockerell. I'm a waiter. I work at a hotel near Loch Ness. I live in a cottage near the hotel. I finish work in the hotel at one o'clock in the morning. Then I walk home with two friends. They work at the hotel, too.

One night in 1988 I worked late. I finished work at two o'clock. I walked home alone, because my friends were already at home. It was a clear night and there was a full moon.

While I was on my way to my cottage, something happened. Something appeared in the lake. It was large and black. I stopped and looked at it. The thing moved along the lake. I watched it for about a minute. Then I hurried to my cottage and grabbed my camera.

But when I returned to the lake, there was nothing there.

I'm sure it was the Loch Ness monster. It was Nessie. I know it was.

The past simple tense

BUILD UP

2 a Read the first two paragraphs. Complete this table with the correct form of the verbs.

1988 past	now present
....	work
....	finish
....	walk

b How do we make the past tense? Complete this rule.

> To make the past tense, we add .... to the verb.

c Find more examples of past tense verbs in the story.

3 Read the story and number these pictures in the correct order.

4 Use the pictures. Tell the story.

5 Answer these questions.

- Who is Nessie?
- What is Alan Cockerell's job?
- Why was he alone that night?
- What was the thing like?
- Why hasn't Alan got a photograph of the thing?

6 What do you think?

- Is this the Loch Ness monster?
- Do you believe Alan Cockerell's story?

FOLLOW UP

7 Write Alan's story. Write one sentence about each of the pictures in Exercise 3. Start like this.

Alan finished work at two o'clock. He walked home alone . . .

LISTENING
The Grey Lady

1 Look at the picture. What do you think the story is about?

2 🔲 Listen to the first part of the tape. Answer these questions.

- Who was the ghost?
- What did it do?

3 What do you think happened a long time ago? Look at these pictures and the cues to help you decide.

offer Sir Roger a lot of money
love Lucy
gamble
live in the village
old and ugly
want to marry Lucy
lock Lucy in a room
refuse to marry Lord Griston
own the house
cry
poor
want to marry Thomas Mowbray
need money
jump out of a window
accept Lord Griston's money
young and handsome
rich

4 🔲 Listen to the second part and match the cues to the correct picture.

Lucy Loxley

refuse to marry
Lord Griston
. . . .
. . . .
. . . .
. . . .
. . . .

/ɪd/ **endings**

BUILD UP

 5 a Look at these sentences.

She **shouted** 'No! No! Never!'
He always **needed** money.
Lord Griston **wanted** to marry Lucy.

b Listen to the story of the Grey Lady again. What do you notice about the verbs?

c Complete this rule.

> When the verb ends in .... or ...., we
> pronounce the -ed ending / ɪd /.

d Say these verbs.

watched	wanted	offered	refused
arrested	locked	jumped	needed
shouted	cried	lived	gambled

 6 Use the cues. Say what each person did in the story.

FOLLOW UP

7 Write the story of the Grey Lady.

Sir Roger Loxley

gamble
. . . .
. . . .
. . . .
. . . .
. . . .

Lord Griston

offer Sir Roger
a lot of money
. . . .
. . . .
. . . .
. . . .

Thomas Mowbray

love Lucy
. . . .
. . . .
. . . .
. . . .
. . . .

INTERACTION

 1 Make a play about Lucy Loxley. Your play should have four acts.

Act 1: Thomas and Lucy fall in love.
Act 2: Lord Griston and Sir Roger arrange the marriage.
Act 3: Lucy refuses to marry Lord Griston.
Act 4: Sir Roger locks Lucy up and she jumps out of the window.

a Work in a group of four. Write the dialogue.

b Each person takes one of the roles.

Lucy Loxley	Lord Griston
Sir Roger Loxley	Thomas Mowbray

c Act your play.

FOLLOW UP

 2 Learn your play.

PROJECT
Mysteries

Collect information about some famous mysteries. Here are some topics.

- monsters like the yeti
- UFOs
- ghosts
- mysterious disappearances
- lost cities

Write about the mysteries and illustrate them with pictures and maps.

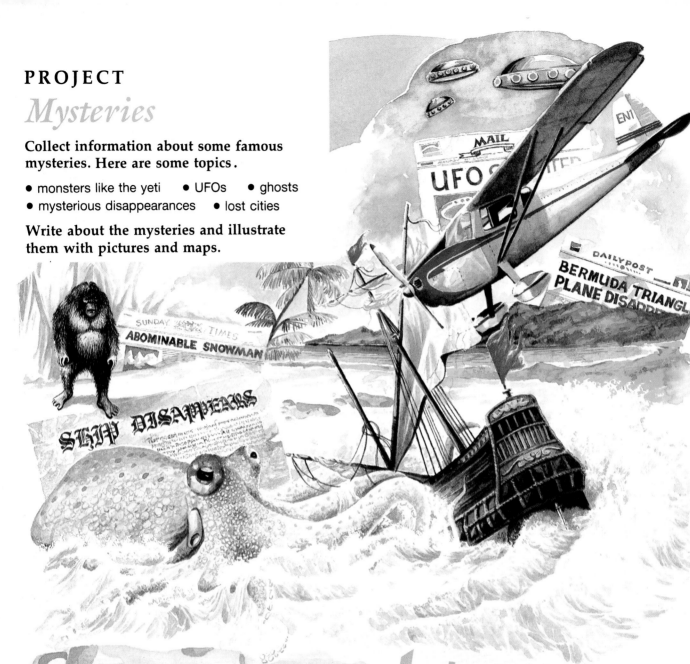

Learning diary

A Look at the first page of this unit. How well do you know these things now? Look at each point in the contents list.

If you know it well, draw a happy face.

If you know it fairly well, draw a face like this.

If you don't know it well, draw a sad face.

B Try the self-check in the Workbook.

C Compare your answers with a partner. Discuss any problems with your teacher.

11

▶ Pronunciation: page 113

12 the news

Contents

Grammar points

The main grammar points in this unit are:

the past simple tense: irregular verbs
Sue went to the cinema.
Casey and Vince found Sue's coat.

the past simple tense: negatives
Sue didn't bring her coat home. Kamala brought it home.
Terry didn't find Sue's coat. Vince and Casey found it.

the past simple tense: questions
What did Terry do with Sue's coat?
Did Vince and Terry find Sue's coat on the grass?

Sue's coat

1 Look at this episode of the story.

- Who are the people?
- Where are they?
- What are they talking about?
- What does Terry do at the end?

(Speech bubble) You come home with Sue Scott every day. Did you come home with her today?

(Speech bubble) No, I didn't. I came home alone. Sue didn't come home.

(Speech bubble) Hi, Kam. What's going on? There's a police car outside. Have you got my coat and...?

(Speech bubble) Sue! You're alive!

(Speech bubble) Oh no! Now I understand. Those three boys. They wanted Terry.

(Speech bubble) You'd better tell us about the three boys, I think.

2 🔊 Listen and follow in your book.

Policewoman You come home with Sue Scott every day. Did you come home with her today?

Kamala No, I didn't. I came home alone. Sue didn't come home. She went to the cinema with some friends. Why?

Casey We found her coat in the lake.

Kamala But Sue didn't have her coat. I had it. I brought it home for her. But I haven't got it now. I . . .

Sue Hi, Kam. What's going on? There's a police car outside. Have you got my coat and . . . ?

Vince and Casey Sue! You're alive!

Later

Policewoman Well, what did you do with the coat?

Kamala I gave it to Terry.

Policewoman And what did he do with it?

Sue I bet he took it to the park and threw it in the lake – the rat!

Kamala No, he didn't do that, Sue. He did something strange. You see, I left him at the corner. When I got to the shop, I could still see him. And he, well . . . ne put your coat on. Oh no! Now I understand. Those three boys. They wanted Terry.

Policewoman You'd better tell us about the three boys, I think.

Later

Kamala So, that's what happened.

Sue Oh, it's all my fault. Poor Terry. Why did I do it?

Vince There he is! At the window.

Casey That's funny. When he saw us, he ran away.

Sue Terry, Terry.

Sue Terry, I'm sorry. I'm sorry.

Terry Oh, hi, you lot.

Why didn't Terry want to see his friends?

3 **Answer these questions.**

a Did Kamala come home with Sue today?
b Where did Sue go after school?
c Who found the coat?
d Why did Sue come to the shop?
e Why didn't Kamala have the coat?
f What did Terry do with the coat?
g Where did Vince see Terry?
h What did Terry do when he saw the others?

The past tense: irregular verbs

 4 This is the regular past tense.

present	past
look	look**ed**

But some verbs have an irregular past tense.

Example

present	past
come	*came*
bring	*brought*
put	*put*

Find the past tense of these verbs in the Victoria Road story.

present	past
come	
have	
see	
take	
go	
find	
give	
leave	
run	
throw	
do	
get	
can	

 5 Listen to the story again and repeat.

Useful expressions

 6 How do you say these in your language?

What's going on?

I bet . . .

The rat!

something strange

You'd better . . .

So that's what happened.

It's all my fault.

There he is!

That's funny.

7 Work in a group of three. One person is Sue and Casey, one is the policewoman and Vince, one is Terry and Kamala. Read the dialogue.

 8 Terry is telling the others what happened. Complete his description with these words.

was	had	walked	went
gave	left	did	saw
took	saw	wanted	
got	put	escaped	

When I .... off the bus, I .... these three guys. Kamala .... on the bus, too. She .... Sue's coat and bags. She .... me the coat and bags. She .... me at the corner and then she .... to her shop. I .... Sue's coat on and .... round the corner. But the three guys .... me. They .... me to the park. They .... to throw me in the lake, but I ....

How .... you escape?

Well ....

LANGUAGE WORK

The past simple tense: negative

BUILD UP

 a **Look at the Victoria Road story. Complete these sentences.**

I .... home alone.

Sue .... home.

Sue .... her coat.

I .... it.

He .... that, Sue.

He .... something strange.

b **How do we make the past simple negative? Complete this rule.**

> To make the past simple negative we put
> .... in front of the infinitive.

c **Complete this table of the past simple negative. Use the correct words from this list.**

find   jumped   didn't   ran   found
did   jump   run

I He She It We You They		
	....	.... away.
	....	.... the coat.
		.... out of the window.

 These statements about the Victoria Road story are all wrong. Correct them.

Example
Sue didn't go to the hospital after school. She went to the cinema.

a Sue went to the hospital after school.
b Kamala brought Vince's coat home.
c She gave the coat to Mrs Scott.
d Terry threw the coat in the lake.
e Vince and Casey found Sue's coat in a tree.
f Terry telephoned the police.
g The policewoman asked Sue about the three boys.
h Vince said, 'It's all my fault'.
i Kamala saw Terry at the shop window.
j Terry came into the shop.

 Imagine that yesterday was the best day of your life.

a **Write down:**
  - six things that you did.
  - six things that you didn't do.

b **Compare your ideas with other people in the class.**

FOLLOW UP

Write your answers to Exercise 2.

JOKE OF THE WEEK

LOCH NESS

IT FOOLS EVERYONE!

READING

Amazing escapes

1 Look at the sentences below. There are three stories here. The sentences are all in the correct order, but the three stories are mixed up. Put A, B or C next to each sentence to make the three stories.

☐ In 1944 Nicholas Alkemade was in a plane over Germany.

☐ A New York man went up the Empire State Building.

☐ In 1989 Thomas Root was on his way from Washington to Florida in a small plane.

☐ He had a heart attack and became unconscious.

☐ He jumped out of a window. But he didn't die.

☐ The German guns hit the plane.

☐ The wind caught him and blew him through another window.

☐ He jumped out of the plane before it exploded.

☐ The plane flew for 1000 miles and then crashed into the sea.

☐ He landed in the NBC television studio in the middle of a programme.

☐ The crash woke him up.

☐ He fell 5485m. He didn't have a parachute.

☐ He landed in some snow in a forest.

☐ He climbed out of the plane before it sank.

☐ The TV presenter interviewed him.

☐ He swam away and a helicopter rescued him.

☐ He didn't break any bones.

☐ He said, 'I changed my mind after I jumped.'

2 How did you sort out the stories? What clues did you use?

W O R D   W O R K

3 a Underline all the verbs in the stories.

b Which verbs are regular?

c Write the past tenses of these irregular verbs.

swim ....   fall ....

catch ....   become ....

say ....   fly ....

wake up ....   sink ....

hit ....

92

FOLLOW UP

 Complete this story.

Vesna Vulovic .... an air stewardess for
Yugoslav Airlines. In 1972 her DC9 plane
.... over Czechoslovakia. She ....
10,160 metres. She .... in a forest. She
.... a lot of bones and ....
unconscious. She .... in hospital for 16
months. But she survived.

LISTENING

Band Aid.....................

 Look at these pictures.

- Who is the man? What do you know about him?
- What do you know about Band Aid?

 Read this text. Try to fill in the missing words.

In the 1970s Bob Geldof .... the singer with

the Boomtown Rats. But in October 1984 his life

.... On the television he ....

pictures of the famine in Ethiopia. Bob Geldof

.... to help. He ....

Band Aid. A group of famous pop stars .... a

record. It was called 'Feed the World'. Bob Geldof

.... to make £70,000 from the record.

It .... £8 million.

Band Aid .... there. In July 1985 Band

Aid .... a pop concert in Britain and America.

The Live Aid concert .... over £60 million.

With the money, Band Aid .... food,

medicine and lorries for the people of Africa.

 ▭ **Listen. You will hear an interview about Band Aid. Complete the text above with the information in the interview.**

FOLLOW UP

Find out more about Band Aid.

- Why was there a famine in Africa?
- Did people in your country help Band Aid? What did they do?

94

INTERACTION

The past simple: questions

BUILD UP

1 a Look at the Victoria Road Story on page 88. Complete these sentences.

.... home with her today?

I .... home alone.

And what .... with it?

He .... something strange.

b Choose the correct words to complete this table.

| went | crashed | go | came |
| crash | made | come | make |

Did	I he she it we you they	.... home alone? .... into the sea? .... £8 million? .... to the cinema?

c Complete the rule.

> To make questions in the past simple we use .... + subject + ...

2 a Listen to the interview about Band Aid again. Complete these questions.

When .... ?

Why .... ?

What .... before he started Band Aid?

What .... first?

How much money .... ?

.... after Feed the World?

What .... called?

b Work with a partner. Use your questions and the text on page 94. Role play the interview.

FOLLOW UP

3 Imagine you have done something interesting. A reporter is interviewing you about it. Write the interview. Use these words.

What?   When?   Why?   Where?   Did?

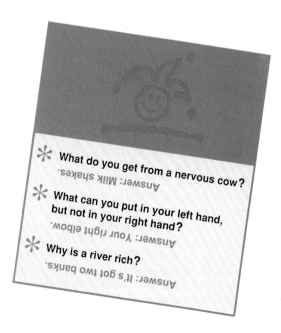

* What do you get from a nervous cow?
Answer: Milk shakes.

* What can you put in your left hand, but not in your right hand?
Answer: Your right elbow.

* Why is a river rich?
Answer: It's got two banks.

PROJECT

A class newspaper

Some English-speaking people are visiting your country. You want to give them some information about what's in the news in your country at the moment.

Make a class newspaper in English. Your newspaper should include a range of stories, for example:

- the main political news in your country
- a world news story
- a human interest story
- a major event, such as a big robbery or a train crash
- sports news

a Decide which area you will work on.

b Watch the television news and read newspapers. Find a good story.

c Write your story in English.

d Illustrate your story with a picture.

e Put all the stories together to make a class newspaper.

f Give your newspaper a name.

Prime Minister Resigns

Crisis at EC Summit

ABBA STAR WEDS

Graf Smashes Way to Second Grand Slam Win

50 Die in Earthquake

★★★

Riots in Two Indian Cities

New Road Opened by Local MP

Learning diary

12

A Look at the first page of this unit. How well do you know these things now? Look at each point in the contents list.

If you know it well, draw a happy face.

If you know it fairly well, draw a face like this.

If you don't know it well, draw a sad face.

B Try the self-check in the Workbook.

C Compare your answers with a partner. Discuss any problems with your teacher.

► Pronunciation: page 114

Contents

Grammar points

The main grammar points in this unit are:

adjectives and adverbs

It was an easy fight.

I escaped easily.

ordinal numbers

dates

12 September
20 March 1975

Terry's story

1 Look at the story.

- What happened in the last episode?
- Who are the people in this episode?
- Where are they?
- What is Terry talking about?
- Why does Vince say 'That's funny'?

> Tell us again, Terry. What happened?

> They caught me easily and they took me to the park.

> They wanted to throw me in the lake, but I pulled hard and the coat came off.

> Then I turned round quickly. I pushed the first boy into the lake. I kicked the second boy and hit the third boy with Sue's bag.

2 📼 Listen and follow in your books.

Casey Tell us again, Terry. What happened?

Terry Well, Darren Tooley and his two friends saw me. I couldn't run very fast, because I had the bags. They caught me easily and they took me to the park. I thought quickly and on the way to the park I unbuttoned the coat carefully.

Kamala Ooh, it's exciting. Just like the movies. What did you do when you got to the park?

Terry They wanted to throw me in the lake. But I pulled hard and the coat came off. Then I turned round quickly. I pushed the first boy into the lake. I kicked the second boy and hit the third boy with Sue's bag. Then they ran away.

Kamala You did very well, Terry. You were so brave.

Terry Oh, it was an easy fight. They fought very badly. But I'm sorry about your coat and bags, Sue.

Sue Oh, that's all right, Terry.

Casey Don't look now, but Tooley and his friends are coming out of the cinema.

Darren Hi, Terry. It's a great film.
Terry Oh, er, . . . hi . . ., er . . . thanks. Balcony, please.
Vince That's funny. Why were those guys so friendly?

Terry Oh . . . er . . . I don't know. Would anyone like an ice cream?

3 Answer these questions.

a Where are the group going?
b What is Terry talking about?
c Why did Darren Tooley and his friends catch Terry easily?
d What did Terry do on the way to the park?
e How did Terry escape?
f What did he do to the three boys?
g Why was it an easy fight?
h What did Darren Tooley and his friends do, when they came out of the cinema?
i Why was Vince surprised?

4 Listen again and repeat.

Useful expressions

5 **How do you say these in your language?**

It's exciting.

Just like the movies.

The coat came off.

You were so brave.

I'm sorry about . . .

That's all right.

Don't look now, but . . .

Would anyone like a . . .?

6 Work with a partner. One person is Terry, one person takes all the other parts. Read the dialogue.

FOLLOW UP

7 Complete Kamala's diary.

We went .... the cinema today. Terry told .... what happened in the park. .... Tooley and his two friends .... Terry easily. He couldn't run .... fast with Sue's bags. They .... him to the park, but .... the way to the .... Terry unbuttoned the coat .... They wanted to throw Terry .... the lake, but he pulled .... and the coat came .... Then he turned round .... He pushed the .... guy into the lake, ...the second guy and .... the third guy with Sue's .... Then they ran .... Terry was so .... , but he said it was an .... fight, because they fought very ....

We saw Darren Tooley and his .... They came out of the .... They were very .... It was funny. Terry bought us all an ....

99

LANGUAGE WORK

Adverbs

BUILD UP

1 a Look at the Victoria Road story. Complete these sentences.

I couldn't run very ....

They caught me ....

I thought ....

These are adverbs. They describe *how* someone did something.

b Find more adverbs in the story.

2 Look at these pictures. Say what the people are doing and how they are doing it. Choose from these adverbs.

quietly	loudly	bravely	sadly
hard	carefully	slowly	badly
easily	fast		

Example
He is driving fast.

Adverbs and adjectives

BUILD UP

3 a Look.

It was an **easy** fight. They caught me **easily**.

This is an **adjective**. It describes the noun 'fight'. It tells us *what* the fight was *like*.

This is an **adverb**. It describes the verb 'caught'. It tells us *how* they caught him.

b Look at the list of adverbs in Exercises 1 and 2. What do most adverbs end with?

But be careful with these adverbs. Complete this list.

adjective	adverb
fast	....
hard	....
friendly	–
good	....

100

4 **Choose the correct word from the brackets.**

Terry can run .... (good/well)

He couldn't get away from Tooley ....
(easy/easily)

Sue's bags were very ....
(heavy/heavily)

Terry fought .... (brave/bravely)

It was an .... fight. (easy/easily)

Tooley and his friends ran away

.... (quick/quickly)

Ordinal numbers
BUILD UP

5 **a** **Look at the Victoria Road story. Complete these.**

the first boy
the .... boy
the .... boy

We call these ordinal numbers.

b 🔊 **Listen and complete this list.**

1st	first	14th	fourteenth
2nd	second	15th	....
3rd	third	16th	....
4th	fourth	17th	seventeenth
5th	fifth	18th	eighteenth
6th	sixth	19th	....
7th	....	20th	twentieth
8th	eighth	21st	twenty-first
9th	ninth	22nd	....
10th	....		....
11th	eleventh		....
12th	twelfth		....
13th	thirteenth		

c **Listen again and repeat.**

d **Add these to the list.**

23rd   24th   25th

A PUZZLE

6 **a** **What is the word? Find these letters.**

the eighth letter in 'yesterday'
the thirteenth letter of the alphabet
the fourth letter in 'believe'
the third letter in the past tense of 'go'
the fifth letter in the second word of 'post office'
the sixth letter in the plural of 'watch'

b **Use your letters to make a word.**

c **Make a puzzle for another word. Give it to another group. Can they solve your puzzle?**

FOLLOW UP

7 **Write your answers to Exercise 2.**

Save Me

Save ....
Oh won't you .... me?
I .... you baby.
Please .... say maybe.

Why won't you save me ....?
.... save me.

.... me.
Please help me, ...
Oh, please, please
Don't .... maybe.

.... won't you help me now?
Please help ....

Tell me.
Oh won't you .... me.
Tell me you love me.
Please don't say ....
Oh why won't .... tell me now?
Please tell me.

.... me.
Oh won't you love me?
.... love you baby.
Please say .... love me, love me.

Why .... you love me now?
I, you .... , I love you.

READING

1 Look at these pictures.

- Who is the man?
- What do you know about him?

2 a Look at the chart.

date	place	event
1931		
1936		
1939		
1952		
1954		
1955		

b Look through the text. Put these places and events in the correct order in your chart.

Paso Robles	move
Hollywood	die in a car crash
Fairmount, Indiana	make films
Los Angeles	go to live with aunt and uncle
New York	born
Fairmount, Indiana	become an actor

James Dean was a film star. He made only three films. He died in a car crash in September 1955 near Paso Robles in California. He was only twenty-four years old. But in his short life James Dean became the symbol of young people. He was the teenage rebel. For years after he died his studio received 8000 letters a day. His fans couldn't believe that he was really dead. Today he is still a hero for millions of young people.

James Dean was born in February 1931 in Fairmount, Indiana. When Jimmy was five years old, his father got a job in Los Angeles and the family moved to California. Three years later his mother died. Jimmy went back to Fairmount and lived with his aunt and uncle on their farm.

Jimmy loved sport. He was in the school basketball and baseball teams. He also played the clarinet.

He wanted to be an actor and in January 1952 he went to New York. He made some advertisements for Pepsi-Cola, appeared in some television programmes and he also worked in the theatre.

In 1954 James Dean went to Hollywood and he made his first film. *East of Eden* made him a star. His second film was *Rebel Without a Cause*. In his third and last film, *Giant*, he starred with Elizabeth Taylor and Rock Hudson.

In 1955 James Dean was famous. He was rich too – rich enough to buy a fast sports car.

 3 Now read the text carefully. Find this information.

- 2 sports that James Dean played
- his first film
- 2 other films that he made
- 3 things that he did in New York

W O R D   W O R K

 4 Find all the words in the text connected with the word 'actor'.

 5 What do you think?

- Why was James Dean famous?
- What does 'teenage rebel' mean to you?

Dates

B U I L D   U P

 6   Listen and repeat.

January	July
February	August
March	September
April	October
May	November
June	December

A   B I R T H D A Y   S U R V E Y

 7 a Ask people in your class: 'Which month is your birthday in?'

b Make a chart to show how many people in the class have birthdays in each month. Which month has the most?

F O L L O W   U P

8 Use the information in your chart. Write a short biography of James Dean. Start like this.

James Dean was born in Fairmount, Indiana in 1931. In 1936 he went to Los Angeles. His mother died in . . .

The death of James Dean

1 📼 **Here is some more information about James Dean. But a lot of it is wrong. Listen and correct it.**

James Dean loved motor racing and he often took part in sports car races. He drove well.

On 21 August 1954 he bought a new car. It was a Ferrari 590 Spyder. It was gold and he paid $9000 for it. That was a lot of money in those days.

At half past one on Saturday 29 September 1955, he left Hollywood with his new girlfriend. They were on their way to a race at Paso Robles. But they didn't arrive at Paso Robles. At 2.26 Dean's Ferrari crashed into a lorry. The speedometer stopped at 100 mph. The crash broke Dean's neck. At that moment a film star died and a legend was born.

2 Listen again and check your answer.

Dates

3 a **Look.**

> We write 30 September.
> But we say *the thirtieth of* September.

b **Say these.**

16 February	22 June	1 January
20 August	13 September	

4 **You've now got a lot of information about James Dean. Work with a partner. Imagine you are interviewing James Dean on 30 September 1955 before he left Hollywood.**

- Decide what questions you will ask.
- One person is the interviewer, one is James Dean. Act your interview.
- Change roles and ask more questions.

FOLLOW UP

5 Write ten questions and answers from your interview with James Dean.

INTERACTION

At the movies

1 a Put this conversation in the correct order.

☐ Batman III.

☐ Let's go to the movies on Saturday.

☐ Fine. See you outside the cinema at 5.15 on Saturday.

☐ What time does it start?

☐ Who's in it?

☐ Studio 2.

☐ OK. See you there.

☐ Oh, I like him. Where is it on?

☐ OK. Let's go at 5.30.

☐ Michael Keaton.

☐ On Saturday it starts at five past two, 5.30 or 8 o'clock.

☐ Good idea. What's on?

b 📼 Listen and check your answer.

c Act the dialogue.

2 a Look at these film posters.

CANNON MARKET STREET

MICHAEL J. FOX
CHRISTOPHER LLOYD
MARY STEENBURGEN

2.15   5.15   8.15

ODEON HIGH STREET

STARTING MONDAY
"CROCODILE" DUNDEE II

PAUL HOGAN AND LINDA KOZLOWSKI
PERFORMANCES DAILY AT: 2.30 5.00 7.30

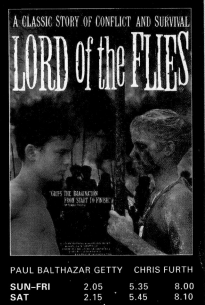

STUDIO ONE

A CLASSIC STORY OF CONFLICT AND SURVIVAL
LORD of the FLIES

PAUL BALTHAZAR GETTY   CHRIS FURTH

SUN–FRI	2.05	5.35	8.00
SAT	2.15	5.45	8.10

b Make dialogues using the posters. Use the dialogue in Exercise 1 as a model.

FOLLOW UP

3 Write one of your dialogues from Exercise 2b.

PROJECT

The movies

Make a project about the movies. Describe these.

- Your favourite films.
- Your favourite actors and actresses.
  What do you know about them?
- The last film that you saw.
  Tell the story. Who was in it? Was it good?

Illustrate your project with pictures.

These two actresses are Rosanna Arquette and Madonna in 'Desperately Seeking Susan'. The film was very funny. I didn't really understand it, but I thought Rosanna Arquette was great. She's now officially my favourite film star. So here's some information about her.

This scene is from 'Top Gun'. The woman is Kelly McGillis and the man is Tom Cruise.

I went to see 'Top Gun' last week. In the film, Tom Cruise was at the United States Navy Fighter Pilots School. He wanted to be the best pilot - the top gun. Kelly McGillis was his teacher at the Pilots School. They fell in love. The story wasn't very good, but the aeroplane scenes were fantastic.

I like Kelly McGillis. I saw her in 'Witness'. It was on the television last year. Harrison Ford was in it, too.

Rosanna Arquette was born in 1959 in the United States. She wasn't the first star in her family. Her grandfather, Clifford Arquette, was an actor, too.

Rosanna became an actress in 1977. She had parts in several TV programmes. She made her first film in 1980. It was called 'More American Graffiti'. Six years later she starred with Madonna in 'Desperately Seeking Susan'.

(I like Madonna, too. She's my favourite singer.)

This is Harrison Ford. I saw him in 'Raiders of the Lost Ark'. I watched it on a video at my friend's house. Harrison Ford played Indiana Jones. It was a great film.

Harrison Ford first became famous, when he played Han Solo in the Star Wars movies. I couldn't find a picture from 'Raiders of the Lost Ark' or 'Star Wars'.

Learning diary

A Look at the first page of this unit. How well do you know these things now? Look at each point in the contents list.

13

If you know it well, draw a happy face.

If you know it fairly well, draw a face like this.

If you don't know it well, draw a sad face.

B Try the self-check in the Workbook.

C Compare your answers with a partner. Discuss any problems with your teacher.

▶ Pronunciation: page 114

14 revision

READING

1 a Look at the picture.

b Read the story. On the picture, draw lines
to show the movements of each person
between 12 o'clock and 2 o'clock.

Ruth Less is a rich woman – or she *was* a rich
woman. On Wednesday 9 June between 1 and 2
o'clock in the morning someone murdered her. The
murderer hit her with a heavy baseball bat.

On 8 June there was a dinner in the evening at
Ruth Less's house. There were four people at the
dinner: Ruth Less; her husband, Dennis; her sister
Cindy Sweet and her business partner, Ken Doe.

The dinner finished at twelve o'clock. At five
past twelve Ken Doe left. He drove home. Cindy
Sweet went to bed. But Ruth Less and her husband
didn't go to bed. Ruth went to her office and

worked. Dennis sat in the living room and read a
book.

At 1 o'clock Ruth Less telephoned Ken Doe.
Dennis Less heard her. He was on his way to bed.
At ten past one Cindy Sweet got up. She couldn't
sleep. She came downstairs. She went into the
living room and watched television.

At 2 o'clock Dennis Less woke up. He heard a
crash downstairs. He came downstairs and he went
into the office. He found Ruth Less on the floor.
She was dead. The French windows were open.
Cindy Sweet was in the kitchen.

2 Mickey Shane, the detective, interviewed Dennis Less. Here are some of the answers he got. What were his questions?

Mickey Shane What time ....?

Dennis Less At twelve o'clock.

Mickey Shane ....?

Dennis Less No, she didn't. Ruth went to her office and worked.

Mickey Shane ....?

Dennis Less No, I didn't. I sat in the living room and read a book.

Mickey Shane ....?

Dennis Less On the floor.

Mickey Shane .... the french windows ....?

Dennis Less Yes, they were but it was a warm night.

Mickey Shane ....?

Dennis Less She was in the kitchen.

 3 Work in pairs. One person is Mickey Shane, one is Dennis Less. Role play the interview.

4 a ▬ Listen. You will hear some more information. Write the new information down.

   b Say what new information you have got.

   Example
   Cindy Sweet didn't like Mrs Less.

5 Can you solve the murder? Who was the murderer? How did he or she do it?

6 ▬ Listen. Mickey Shane is explaining how it happened.

Which of these are important clues?

the glass   a police car
the telephone   the baseball bat
the television   the door handle
fingerprints

FOLLOW UP

7 Describe how the murderer killed Ruth Less.

8 Make your own Whodunnit.

- Describe what happened.
- Draw a plan of the scene.
- Introduce the suspects.
- Make an interview between Mickey Shane and a suspect.

Can other people in the class find the criminal?

a Look at this Top Twenty Chart.
  Do you know any of these songs?
  Translate the titles into your
  own language.

Happy Birthday Radio 581

TOP TWENTY

It's the Hotline programme's birthday today. Here are our Top Twenty requests. These are the twenty most-requested records since Hotline started.

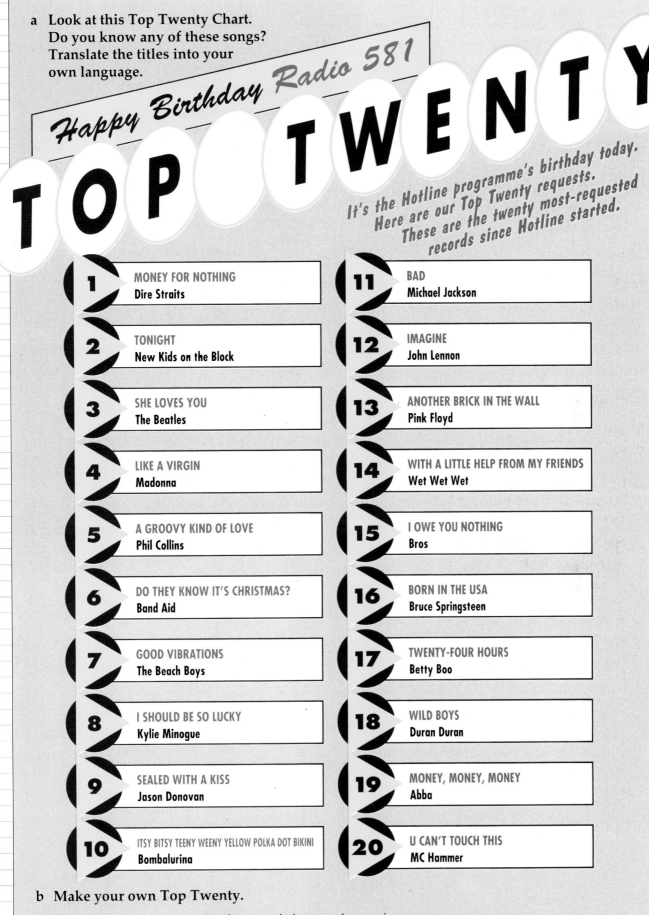

1	MONEY FOR NOTHING Dire Straits	
2	TONIGHT New Kids on the Block	
3	SHE LOVES YOU The Beatles	
4	LIKE A VIRGIN Madonna	
5	A GROOVY KIND OF LOVE Phil Collins	
6	DO THEY KNOW IT'S CHRISTMAS? Band Aid	
7	GOOD VIBRATIONS The Beach Boys	
8	I SHOULD BE SO LUCKY Kylie Minogue	
9	SEALED WITH A KISS Jason Donovan	
10	ITSY BITSY TEENY WEENY YELLOW POLKA DOT BIKINI Bombalurina	

11	BAD Michael Jackson	
12	IMAGINE John Lennon	
13	ANOTHER BRICK IN THE WALL Pink Floyd	
14	WITH A LITTLE HELP FROM MY FRIENDS Wet Wet Wet	
15	I OWE YOU NOTHING Bros	
16	BORN IN THE USA Bruce Springsteen	
17	TWENTY-FOUR HOURS Betty Boo	
18	WILD BOYS Duran Duran	
19	MONEY, MONEY, MONEY Abba	
20	U CAN'T TOUCH THIS MC Hammer	

b **Make your own Top Twenty.**

● Find out the twenty most popular records in your class or in your group.
● Translate the titles into English.
● Write your chart in English.

▶ Pronunciation: page 114

1 a Look back at the Victoria Road stories. Make a final episode for it.

b Role play your story.

2 🔊 Listen. You will hear how the story ends. Compare your story to the real one.

Learning diary

14

You've come to the end of this book. But it's not the end of learning English.

How do you feel about the things that you have learnt? Look back at the Learning diaries in the book. Write down:

- 3 things that you know well now.
- 3 things that you are still not sure about.
- 3 things that you really enjoyed.
- 3 things that you didn't like much.

Discuss your lists with other members of your class. How do you learn best?

What can you do to learn the things you are not sure about?

Good luck with your next year of English!

VICTORIA ROAD

▶ **Pronunciation: page 114**

PRONUNCIATION PRACTICE

Unit 1 Vowels

a Look.

We write	We say
he	/ hi: /
two	/ tu: /
I	/ aɪ /

These are *phonetic* symbols.

b Use the wordlist on page 115. Write these words with phonetic symbols.

pop   ....

desk   ....

bag   ....

book   ....

Britain   ....

door   ....

c Complete these words with phonetic symbols. Check your answers in the wordlist.

from	/fr .... m/
five	/f ..... v/
pen	/p .... n/
we	/w ... /
four	/f .... /
who	/h .... /

Consonants

Look.

We write	We say
bag	/ bæg /
desk	/ desk /

But some consonants have special phonetic symbols.

this	/ ðɪs /
three	/ θri:/
teacher	/ ˈti:tʃə (r)/

Find the words below in the wordlist on page 115. What are the symbols for the underlined letters?

she   you   orange   six   just

....

Find other words with these symbols.

Unit 2 Spelling

In English the spelling and the sound are not always the same.

Look.

different spelling	same sound
you	/ ju: /
two	/ tu: /

same spelling	different sound
book	/ bʊk /
door	/dɔ:(r)/

Find two more examples.

Compare this to your own language.

/ h /

a 📼 Listen and repeat.

he his how her here Hartfield hamburger hello

b Say these.

How old is he?   Can I help you?
Is this her hamburger?   Is he here?

Unit 3 /ɒ/, /ɔ:/

a 🔊 Listen to the numbers and the words. If the word has an /ɔ:/ sound, tick the box.

b Join up the ticks from the lowest number to the highest number. What shape do you get?

☐ 6
10 ☐   ☐ 7
☐ 8
4 ☐   ☐ 13
☐ 5
12
9 ☐   ☐   ☐ 14
☐ 3
☐ 2   ☐ 1
11 ☐

Unit 4 /æ/, /ɑ:/

a 🔊 Listen and repeat.

/æ/	/ɑ:/
van	car
Maths	past
apple	answer

b 🔊 Listen and put these words in the van or the car.

badge   dance   black   flat
Saturday   class   dark   can   can't

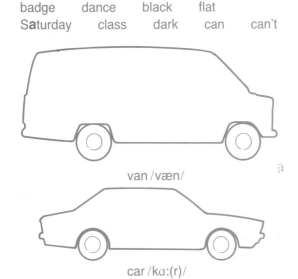

van /væn/

car /kɑ:(r)/

c Say all the words.

Unit 5 /æ/, /ʌ/

a Listen and put these words in the front garden or the back garden.

cupboard   come   must   at
touch   cafe   up   number
garage   that   flat   badge

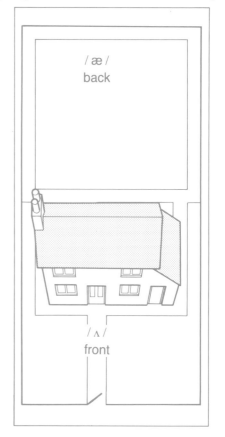

/æ/
back

/ʌ/
front

b Listen again and repeat.

Unit 6 Revision

Write this dialogue in words.

ˌkæn aɪ ˈhelp juː

....

ə ˌtʃiːzbɜːgə ænd ən ˈɒrɪndʒ dʒuːs pliːz

....

ˌenɪθɪŋ ˈels

....

nəʊ ˈθæŋk juː

....

ðæts ˌwʌn paʊnd ˈθɜːti tuː pliːz

....

112

Unit 7 /ɒ/, /əʊ/

a 🔊 **Listen. If you hear the /ɒ/ sound, say STOP. If you hear the /əʊ/ sound, say GO.**

stop	smoke	long	know
go	clock	d**o**ctor	on
shop	home	c**o**la	don't
close	watch	ch**o**colate	road
open	goal	not	p**o**p star

b 🔊 **Listen again. Put the words in the correct box.**

stop / ɒ /	go / əʊ /

c Say the words.

Unit 8 /u:/, /ju:/

a 🔊 **Listen and repeat.**

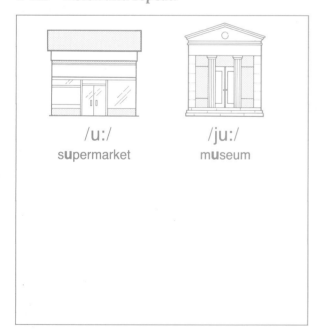

/u:/
s**u**permarket

/ju:/
m**u**seum

b 🔊 **Listen and put these words under the supermarket or the museum.**

do	choose	st**u**dent	exc**u**se me
room	blue	m**u**sic	n**ew**spaper
Tuesday	s**ou**venir	f**oo**d	swimming p**oo**l
comp**u**ter	n**ew**	comm**u**nity work	

c Say all the words.

Unit 9 Unstressed /ə/

a 🔊 **Listen and repeat.**

scissors trousers sweater summer
souvenir magazine corner photograph
understand hamburger

b Underline the syllable with the /ə/ sound.

c Say the words.

Unit 10 Revision

Write this dialogue in words.

də jə ˌlaɪk ðɪs ˈtiːʃɜːt

....

nəʊ ˌaɪ ˈdəʊnt bʌt ˌaɪ ˈlaɪk ðəʊz ˈdʒiːnz

....

haʊ ˈmʌtʃ ɑː ðeɪ

....

ðeə ˌθɜːti fɔː ˈpaʊnz

....

əʊ ˌðæts veri ɪkˈspensɪv

....

Unit 11 /ɪ/, /iː/

🔊 **Who is this? Listen and join the dots in the correct order.**

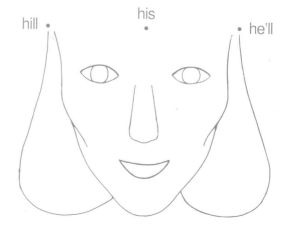

this •   • he's   • live

these •   leave •

hill •   his   • he'll
                  •

113

Unit 12 / v /

🔊 **Listen and repeat.**

village	have	visit	give
voice	living room	love	interview
souvenir	river	heavy	favourite

Unit 13 / ɜː /

🔊 **Listen and repeat.**

bird	world	word
first	thirty-first	work
weren't	early	were

Unit 14 Revision

Write this dialogue in words.

ˌaɪ sɔː əˈɡəʊst ɪn ðɪs ruːm jestədɪ

....

ˌwɒt wəz ɪt ˈlaɪk

....

ɪt wəz ə ˌjʌŋ ˈwʊmən wɪð ˌlɒŋ ˈheə

....

ˌwɒt dɪd ʃiː ˈduː

....

ʃiː keɪm θruː ˌðæt ˈwɔːl bʌt ˌðen ʃiː ˌdɪsəˈpɪəd

....

ˌhuː ˈwɒz ʃiː

....

ˌaɪ dəʊnt ˈnəʊ

....

WORDLIST

UNIT 1
INTRODUCTION
hello /hə'ləʊ/
hi /haɪ/
what /wɒt/
name /neɪm/
from /frɒm/
Britain /'brɪtən/
Australia /ɒ'streɪlɪə/

---

the USSR /ðə ˌjuː es es
  'ɑː(r)/
the USA /ðə ˌjuː es 'eɪ/
the States /ðə 'steɪts/
the Philippines /ðə
  'fɪlɪpiːnz/
Argentina /ˌɑːdʒən'tiːnə/
Brazil /brə'zɪl/
Spain /speɪn/
Germany /'dʒɜːmənɪ/
Greece /griːs/
Italy /'ɪtəlɪ/
famous /'feɪməs/
favourite /'feɪvərɪt/
pop star /'pɒp ˌstɑː(r)/
sports star /'spɔːts stɑː(r)/

---

desk /desk/
pen /pen/
pencil /'pensl/
window /'wɪndəʊ/
blackboard /'blækbɔːd/
teacher /'tiːtʃə(r)/
book /bʊk/
bag /bæg/
cassette recorder /kə'set
  rɪkɔːdə(r)/
door /dɔː(r)/

---

fast /fɑːst/
alphabet /'ælfəbet/
car /kɑː(r)/
cabriolet /ˌkæbrɪə'leɪ/
convertible /kən'vɜːtəbl/
this /ðɪs/

---

radio /'reɪdɪəʊ/
programme /'prəʊgræm/
DJ /'diː ˌdʒeɪ/
on the line /ˌɒn ðə 'laɪn/
boyfriend /'bɔɪfrend/
girlfriend /'gɜːlfrend/
record (noun) /'rekɔːd/
birthday /'bɜːθdeɪ/
today /tə'deɪ/
happy /'hæpɪ/
Who . . . ? /hu: . . ./
How old . . . ? /haʊ 'əʊld
  . . ./
I don't know. /aɪ ˌdəʊnt
  'nəʊ/
I think . . . /aɪ 'θɪŋk . . ./
thank you /'θæŋk ju:/

---

fast food /fɑːst 'fuːd/
hamburger /'hæmbɜːgə(r)/
cheeseburger /'tʃiːzbɜːgə(r)/
eggburger /'egbɜːgə(r)/
french fries /ˌfrentʃ 'fraɪz/
juice /dʒuːs/

apple /'æpl/
orange /'ɒrɪndʒ/
cola /'kəʊlə/
p (pence) /pens/
£ (pound) /paʊnd/
egg /eg/
Can I help you? /ˌkən aɪ
  'help ju:/
Anything else? /ˌenɪθɪŋ
  'els/
please /pliːz/

What's this called? /wɒts
  'ðɪs kɔːld/
What does . . . mean?
  /wɒt dʌz '. . . miːn/
How do you say . . . ?
  /ˌhaʊ də ju: seɪ '. . ./
in English /ɪn 'ɪŋglɪʃ/
pronounce /prə'naʊns/
spell /spel/
just /dʒʌst/

UNIT 2 YOU
rap /ræp/
Pleased to meet
  you. /ˌpliːzd tə 'miːt ju:/
How do you do? /ˌhaʊ də
  ju: 'du:/
another /ə'nʌðə(r)/
football /'fʊtbɔːl/
game /geɪm/
call /kɔːl/
sing /sɪŋ/
song /sɒŋ/
add /æd/

---

new /njuː/
neighbour /'neɪbə(r)/
brother /'brʌðə(r)/
boy /bɔɪ/
girl /gɜːl/
twins /twɪnz/
friend /frend/
best /best/
See you. /'siː ju:/
next door /nekst 'dɔː(r)/
What are they like? /ˌwɒt
  ɑː(r) ðeɪ 'laɪk/
all right /'ɔːl raɪt/
sister /'sɪstə(r)/
a bit /ə 'bɪt/
bossy /'bɒsɪ/
not /nɒt/
You just wait. /ˌju: dʒʌst
  'weɪt/
quiet /'kwaɪət/

---

good /gʊd/
fan /fæn/
singer /'sɪŋə(r)/
great /greɪt/
rubbish /'rʌbɪʃ/
wonderful /'wʌndəfl/
bad /bæd/
terrible /'terəbl/
very /'verɪ/
awful /'ɔːfl/
OK /əʊ'keɪ/
group /gruːp/

---

leisure centre /'leʒə(r)
  ˌsentə(r)/

age /eɪdʒ/
address /ə'dres/
road /rəʊd/
telephone /'telɪfəʊn/
number /'nʌmbə(r)/
How do you spell
  . . . ? /ˌhaʊ də jɔ: spel
  '. . ./
double /'dʌbl/

T-shirt /'tiː ʃɜːt/
each /iːtʃ/
How much . . . ? /haʊ
  'mʌtʃ . . ./
shop /ʃɒp/
postcard /'pəʊstkɑːd/
small /smɔːl/
large /lɑːdʒ/
Can I have . . . ? /kən aɪ
  hæv '. . ./
I'll take it. /aɪl 'teɪk ɪt/
altogether /ˌɔːltə'geðə(r)/
Here you are. /'hɪə ju:
  ɑː(r)/
change /tʃeɪndʒ/
umbrella /ʌm'brelə/
badge /bædʒ/
tracksuit /'træksuːt/
watch /wɒtʃ/
red /red/
black /blæk/
green /griːn/
white /waɪt/
yellow /'jeləʊ/
blue /bluː/
customer /'kʌstəmə(r)/
sales assistant /'seɪlz
  əsɪstənt/

UNIT 3 PEOPLE
fair /feə(r)/
dark /dɑːk/
hair /heə(r)/
eye /aɪ/
brown /braʊn/
tall /tɔːl/
short /ʃɔːt/
date /deɪt/
Saturday /'sætədɪ/
colour /'kʌlə(r)/
long /lɒŋ/
blond /blɒnd/
pretty /'prɪtɪ/
secret /'siːkrɪt/
big /bɪg/
guy /gaɪ/
What are you up to? /wɒt
  ɑː ju: 'ʌp tuː/
school /skuːl/
Wait and see. /ˌweɪt ænd
  'siː/

---

son /sʌn/
daughter /'dɔːtə(r)/
mother /'mʌðə(r)/
father /'fɑːðə(r)/
wife /waɪf/
husband /'hʌzbənd/
parents /'peərənts/
grandparents
  /'grændpeərənts/
family /'fæməlɪ/

grandmother /ˈgrændmʌðə(r)/
grandfather /ˈgrændfɑːðə(r)/
grandson /ˈgrændsʌn/
granddaughter /ˈgrændɔːtə(r)/
prince /prɪns/
princess /prɪnˈses/
queen /kwiːn/
captain /ˈkæptɪn/

It's time for . . . /ɪts ˌtaɪm fɔː ˈ. . ./
blind date /ˌblaɪnd ˈdeɪt/
ready /ˈredɪ/
possible /ˈpɒsəbl/
job /dʒɒb/
student /ˈstjuːdənt/
shop assistant /ˈʃɒp əsɪstənt/
Scotland /ˈskɒtlənd/
engineer /endʒəˈnɪə(r)/
choose /tʃuːz/
nice /naɪs/
voice /vɔɪs/
boring /ˈbɔːrɪŋ/
fun /fʌn/
bank manager /ˈbæŋk mænɪdʒə(r)/
doctor /ˈdɒktə(r)/
farmer /ˈfɑːmə(r)/
footballer /ˈfʊtbɔːlə(r)/
policeman /pəˈliːsmən/

walkman /ˈwɔːkmən/
house /haʊs/
flat /flæt/
computer /kɒmˈpjuːtə(r)/
dictionary /ˈdɪkʃənrɪ/
often /ˈɒfn/
want /wɒnt/
first /fɜːst/
information /ˌɪnfəˈmeɪʃn/
need /niːd/
photograph /ˈfəʊtəgrɑːf/
basic /ˈbeɪsɪk/
male /meɪl/
female /ˈfiːmeɪl/
lastly /ˈlɑːstlɪ/
yourself /jɔːˈself/
good-looking /ˌgʊd ˈlʊkɪŋ/
shy /ʃaɪ/
honest /ˈɒnɪst/
strike /straɪk/
once /wʌns/
even /ˈiːvn/
likes and dislikes /ˌlaɪks ən ˈdɪslaɪks/
least /liːst/
worst /wɜːst/
food /fuːd/
think /θɪŋk/
world /wɜːld/
idea /aɪˈdɪə/
the opposite sex /ðiː ˌɒpəzɪt ˈseks/
ideal /aɪˈdɪəl/
interesting /ˈɪntrəstɪŋ/
intelligent /ɪnˈtelɪdʒənt/
friendly /ˈfrendlɪ/
happy /ˈhæpɪ/
was /wɒz/, /wəz/

writer /ˈraɪtə(r)/
never /ˈnevə(r)/
could /kʊd/, /kəd/

UNIT 4 TIME
dance /dɑːns/
that /ðæt/
over there /ˌəʊvə ˈðeə(r)/
really /ˈrɪəlɪ/
near /nɪə(r)/
see /siː/
with /wɪð/
Go on. /gəʊ ɒn/
Excuse me. /ɪksˈkjuːz miː/
Would you like to . . .? /ˌwəd ju ˈlaɪk tə . . ./
I'm sorry. /aɪm ˈsɒrɪ/
everybody /ˈevrɪbɒdɪ/
I mean . . . /aɪ ˈmiːn . . ./
hear /hɪə(r)/
stupid /ˈstjuːpɪd/
answer /ˈɑːnsə(r)/
face /feɪs/
so /səʊ/
funny /ˈfʌnɪ/
table /ˈteɪbl/

can /kən/, /kæn/
can't /kɑːnt/
play /pleɪ/
guitar /gɪˈtɑː(r)/
speak /spiːk/
English /ˈɪŋglɪʃ/
swim /swɪm/
read /riːd/
music /ˈmjuːzɪk/
badminton /ˈbædmɪntən/
ski /skiː/
drive /draɪv/

timetable /ˈtaɪmteɪbl/
subject (noun) /ˈsʌbdʒɪkt/
period /ˈpɪərɪəd/
homework /ˈhəʊmwɜːk/
RE /ɑː ˈriː/
French /frentʃ/
Science /ˈsaɪəns/
Maths /mæθs/
Technology /tekˈnɒlədʒɪ/
History /ˈhɪstrɪ/
Geography /dʒɪˈɒgrəfɪ/
PE /ˌpiː ˈiː/
Art /ɑːt/
lunch /lʌntʃ/
break /breɪk/
assembly /əˈsemblɪ/
registration /redʒɪˈstreɪʃn/

clock /klɒk/
to /tə/, /tuː/
o'clock /əˈklɒk/
past /pɑːst/
minute /ˈmɪnɪt/
time /taɪm/
on /ɒn/
at /ət/, /æt/

appointment /əˈpɔɪntmənt/
dentist /ˈdentɪst/
next /nekst/
afternoon /ˌɑːftəˈnuːn/
morning /ˈmɔːnɪŋ/

come /kʌm/
after /ˈɑːftə(r)/
fine /faɪn/
goodbye /ˌgʊdˈbaɪ/
van /væn/

UNIT 5 PLACES
go /gəʊ/
angry /ˈæŋgrɪ/
still /stɪl/
with /wɪð/
late /leɪt/
tomorrow /təˈmɒrəʊ/
See you. /ˈsiː juː/
chocolate /ˈtʃɒklət/
milk shake /ˈmɪlk ʃeɪk/
talk /tɔːk/
silly /ˈsɪlɪ/
put /pʊt/
tray /treɪ/
touch /tʌtʃ/
careful /ˈkeəfl/
drink /drɪŋk/
again /əˈgen/
Get out of the way. /ˌget aʊt əv ðə ˈweɪ/
cafe /ˈkæfeɪ/
seat /siːt/

stand up /stænd ˈʌp/
sit down /sɪt ˈdaʊn/
write /raɪt/
look /lʊk/
pick up /pɪk ˈʌp/
close /kləʊz/
open /ˈəʊpən/
picture /ˈpɪktʃə(r)/

disk /dɪsk/
disk drive /ˈdɪsk draɪv/
monitor /ˈmɒnɪtə(r)/
screen /skriːn/
keyboard /ˈkiːbɔːd/
part /pɑːt/
keep /kiːp/
envelope /ˈenvələʊp/
ballpoint pen /ˈbɔːlpɔɪnt ˈpen/
between /bɪˈtwiːn/
magnet /ˈmægnɪt/
carefully /ˈkeəfəlɪ/
must /məst/, /mʌst/
mustn't /ˈmʌsnt/
bit /bɪt/
kilobyte /ˈkɪləbaɪt/
VDU /ˌviː diː ˈjuː/
visual display unit /ˌvɪʒʊəl dɪˈspleɪ juːnɪt/
hardware /ˈhɑːdweə(r)/
software /ˈsɒftweə(r)/
mouse /maʊs/
floppy disk /ˈflɒpɪ dɪsk/
hard disk /ˈhɑːd dɪsk/
supermarket /ˈsuːpəmɑːkɪt/
disco /ˈdɪskəʊ/
bar /bɑː(r)/
toilet /ˈtɔɪlɪt/
goal /gəʊl/
up /ʌp/
shop /ʃɒp/
sandwich /ˈsændwɪdʒ/
jumbo jet /ˌdʒʌmbəʊ ˈdʒet/

pizza /'pi:tsə/
film /fɪlm/
pop music /'pɒp mju:zɪk/
sport /spɔ:t/
hi-fi /'haɪ faɪ/
stereo /'steriəʊ/
video /'vɪdiəʊ/
jeans /dʒi:nz/
coffee /'kɒfɪ/
menu /'menju:/
restaurant /'restrɒnt/
football /'fʊtbɔ:l/

dining room /'daɪnɪŋ
    ru:m/
upstairs /ˌʌp'steəz/
living room /'lɪvɪŋ ru:m/
downstairs /ˌdaʊn'steəz/
bathroom /'bɑ:θru:m/
hall /hɔ:l/
stairs /steəz/
garage /'gærɑ:ʒ,
    /'gærɪdʒ/
bedroom /'bedru:m/
garden /'gɑ:dn/
front /frʌnt/
back /bæk/
cellar /'selə(r)/
toilet /'tɔɪlɪt/
kitchen /'kɪtʃən/
loo /lu:/
cupboard /'kʌbəd/
outside /aʊt'saɪd/
How many . . .? /haʊ
    'menɪ . . ./
balcony /'bælkənɪ/

Have a drink. /ˌhæv ə
    'drɪŋk/
How can you tell
    . . .? /ˌhaʊ kən ju: 'tel
    . . ./
elephant /'elɪfənt/
been /bi:n/
fridge /frɪdʒ/
footprint /'fʊtprɪnt/

UNIT 6 REVISION
dancer /'dɑ:nsə(r)/
home /həʊm/
lesson /'lesn/
only /'əʊnlɪ/
both /bəʊθ/
stone /stəʊn/
cold /kəʊld/
baby /'beɪbɪ/
belong to /bɪ'lɒŋ tə/
dream /dri:m/
ticket /'tɪkɪt/
ride /raɪd/
train /treɪn/
heart /hɑ:t/
square /skweə(r)/
try /traɪ/

UNIT 7 SPORT
know /nəʊ/
live /lɪv/
go to school /ˌgəʊ tə 'sku:l/
other /'ʌðə(r)/
get /get/
bus /bʌs/
every day /ˌevrɪ 'deɪ/

helpful /'helpfl/
about /ə'baʊt/
surprise /sə'praɪz/
table tennis /'teɪbl tenɪs/

goalkeeper /'gəʊlki:pə(r)/
the rest of . . . /ðə 'rest əv
    . . ./
week /wi:k/
weekend /ˌwi:'kend/
go out with . . . /gəʊ 'aʊt
    wɪð . . ./
go to work /ˌgəʊ tə 'wɜ:k/
work /wɜ:k/
bank /bæŋk/
get up /get 'ʌp/
golf /gɒlf/
club /klʌb/
team /ti:m/
practise /'præktɪs/
player /'pleɪə(r)/
show /ʃəʊ/
video /'vɪdiəʊ/
manager /'mænɪdʒə(r)/
match /mætʃ/
watch /wɒtʃ/
breakfast /'brekfəst/
start /stɑ:t/

unusual /ʌn'ju:ʒl/
day /deɪ/
skating rink /'skeɪtɪŋ rɪŋk/
ice skater /'aɪs skeɪtə(r)/
shower /'ʃaʊə(r)/
get dressed /get 'drest/
tea /ti:/
cinema /'sɪnəmɑ:/
early /'ɜ:lɪ/
evening /'i:vnɪŋ/
take /teɪk/
stay /steɪ/
night /naɪt/
go to bed /ˌgəʊ tə 'bed/
till /tɪl/
television /'telɪvɪʒn/
disco /'dɪskəʊ/
catch /kætʃ/
finish /'fɪnɪʃ/
sleep /sli:p/
get out of /get 'aʊt əv/
same /seɪm/
every /'evrɪ/
get home /get 'həʊm/
each /i:tʃ/
How long . . .? / haʊ 'lɒŋ
    . . ./
How often . . .? /haʊ 'ɒfn
    . . ./
grow up /grəʊ 'ʌp/
next /nekst/
first /fɜ:st/
last /lɑ:st/
get into /get 'ɪntu:/
survey (noun) /'sɜ:veɪ/
smoke /sməʊk/

sport /spɔ:t/
sports event /spɔ:ts ɪ'vent/
TV /ˌti: 'vi:/

UNIT 8 TIME OUT
film /fɪlm/

let's /lets/
join /dʒɔɪn/
help /help/
shop /ʃɒp/
community work
    /kə'mju:nətɪ wɜ:k/
hospital /'hɒspɪtl/
coat /kəʊt/
in a hurry /ˌɪn ə 'hʌrɪ/
It doesn't matter. /ɪt
    ˌdʌznt 'mætə(r)/
nobody /'nəʊbədɪ/
a driving lesson /ə 'draɪvɪŋ
    lesn/
give /gɪv/
heavy /'hevɪ/
wait /weɪt/
miss /mɪs/
or /ɔ:(r)/
if /ɪf/
thanks /θæŋks/
love /lʌv/

beach /bi:tʃ/
hill /hɪl/
island /'aɪlənd/
forest /'fɒrɪst/
bridge /brɪdʒ/
river /'rɪvə(r)/
sea /si:/
restaurant /'restrɒnt/
supermarket
    /'su:pəmɑ:kɪt/
post office /'pəʊst ɒfɪs/
souvenir /ˌsu:və'nɪə(r)/
tennis court /'tenɪs kɔ:t/
swimming pool /'swɪmɪŋ
    pu:l/
hut /hʌt/
village /'vɪlɪdʒ/
wonderful /'wʌndəfl/
picnic /'pɪknɪk/
climb /klaɪm/
fish /fɪʃ/
send /send/
letter /'letə(r)/
buy /baɪ/
food /fu:d/
clothes /kləʊðz/
go windsurfing /gəʊ
    'wɪndsɜ:fɪŋ/
go walking /gəʊ 'wɔ:kɪŋ/
go skating /gəʊ 'skeɪtɪŋ/
go skiing /gəʊ 'ski:ɪŋ/

museum /mju:'zi:əm/
snake /sneɪk/
church /tʃɜ:tʃ/
shark /ʃɑ:k/
tiger /'taɪgə(r)/
castle /'kɑ:sl/
insect /'ɪnsekt/
horse /hɔ:s/
dog /dɒg/
lion /'laɪən/
sometimes /'sʌmtaɪmz/
always /'ɔ:lweɪz/
usually /'ju:ʒəlɪ/
interesting /'ɪntrəstɪŋ/
building /'bɪldɪŋ/
city /'sɪtɪ/
clean /kli:n/

expensive /ɪkˈspensɪv/
spider /ˈspaɪdə(r)/

ticket /ˈtɪkɪt/
have a rest /ˌhæv ə ˈrest/
go swimming /ɡəʊ
   ˈswɪmɪŋ/
unforgettable
   /ˌʌnfəˈɡetəbl/
fine /faɪn/
hotel /həʊˈtel/
Kenyan /ˈkenjən/
coast /kəʊst/
worry /ˈwʌrɪ/
sunbathe /ˈsʌnbeɪð/
beautiful /ˈbjuːtɪfl/
lie /laɪ/
sand /sænd/
warm /wɔːm/
water /ˈwɔːtə(r)/
highest /ˈhaɪɪst/
visit /ˈvɪzɪt/
Indian Ocean /ˌɪndɪən
   ˈəʊʃn/
spend /spend/
dhow /daʊ/
safari /səˈfɑːrɪ/
Africa /ˈæfrɪkə/
national park /ˌnæʃnəl
   ˈpɑːk/
elephant /ˈelɪfənt/
giraffe /dʒɪˈrɑːf/
zebra /ˈzebrə/
flamingo /fləˈmɪŋɡəʊ/
forget /fəˈget/
camera /ˈkæmrə/
mountain /ˈmaʊntɪn/
newspaper
   /ˈnjuːspeɪpə(r)/

UNIT 9 CLOTHES

those /ðəʊz/
carry /ˈkærɪ/
explain /ɪkˈspleɪn/
What's the matter? /ˌwɒts
   ðə ˈmætə(r)/
hide /haɪd/
round the corner /ˌraʊnd
   ðə ˈkɔːnə(r)/
sweater /ˈswetə(r)/
jeans /dʒiːnz/
jacket /ˈdʒækɪt/
trousers /ˈtraʊzəz/
sweatshirt /ˈswet-ʃɜːt/
sit /sɪt/
wall /wɔːl/
wind /wɪnd/
blow /bləʊ/
hood /hʊd/
quick /kwɪk/
chase /tʃeɪs/
arrive /əˈraɪv/

cook /kʊk/
eat /iːt/
cut /kʌt/
bread /bred/
magazine /ˌmæɡəˈziːn/

clothes /kləʊðz/
pink /pɪŋk/
jumper /ˈdʒʌmpə(r)/
skirt /skɜːt/

tights /taɪts/
shoes /ʃuːz/
purple /ˈpɜːpl/
headband /ˈhedbænd/
gloves /glʌvz/
suit /suːt/
by /baɪ/
shirt /ʃɜːt/
belt /belt/
dress /dres/
earrings /ˈɪərɪŋz/
bracelet /breɪslɪt/
jewel /ˈdʒuːəl/
silver /ˈsɪlvə(r)/
sporty /ˈspɔːtɪ/
brooch /brəʊtʃ/
price /praɪs/
maybe /ˈmeɪbiː/
shorts /ʃɔːts/
orange /ˈɒrɪndʒ/
grey /greɪ/
waistcoat /ˈweɪskəʊt/
canvas /ˈkænvəs/
outfit /ˈaʊtfɪt/
cricket /ˈkrɪkt/
socks /sɒks/
baseball /ˈbeɪsbɔːl/
boots /buːts/
hold /həʊld/
cap /kæp/
hand /hænd/
cheap /tʃiːp/
trainers /ˈtreɪnəz/
housework /ˈhaʊswɜːk/
wedding /ˈwedɪŋ/
lorry /ˈlɒrɪ/
thought /θɔːt/
round /raʊnd/
ragged /ˈræɡɪd/
rock /rɒk/
rascal /ˈrɑːskl/
ran /ræn/
before /bɪˈfɔː(r)/
go to bed /ˌɡəʊ tə ˈbed/

these /ðiːz/
scissors /ˈsɪzəz/
understand /ˌʌndəˈstænd/
kids /kɪdz/
today /təˈdeɪ/

Can I try them on? /kən aɪ
   ˌtraɪ ðem ˈɒn/
of course /əv ˈkɔːs/
changing room /ˈtʃeɪndʒɪŋ
   ruːm/
fine /faɪn/

sunglasses /ˈsʌnglɑːsɪz/
tie /taɪ/
hat /hæt/
scarf /skɑːf/
scarves /skɑːvz/
necklace /ˈneklɪs/
baby /ˈbeɪbɪ/
doll /dɒl/
boogie /ˈbuːɡɪ/
all night long /ˌɔːl naɪt
   ˈlɒŋ/
teens /tiːnz/
diamond /ˈdaɪəmənd/
ring /rɪŋ/
shake /ʃeɪk/

thing /θɪŋ/

UNIT 10 REVISION

day /deɪ/
miles /maɪlz/
collect /kəˈlekt/
water /ˈwɔːtə(r)/
clean /kliːn/
fetch /fetʃ/
bottle /ˈbɒtl/
stamp /stæmp/
sell /sel/
send /send/
money /ˈmʌnɪ/
tools /tuːlz/
materials /məˈtɪərɪəlz/
build /bɪld/
pipe /paɪp/
frog /frɒg/
after /ˈɑːftə(r)/
someone /ˈsʌmwʌn/
before /bɪˈfɔː(r)/

UNIT 11 MYSTERY

nil /nɪl/
second /ˈsekənd/
brilliant /ˈbrɪlɪənt/
grass /grɑːs/
bench /bentʃ/
park /pɑːk/
lake /leɪk/
someone /ˈsʌmwʌn/
on our way back /ˌɒn ɑː
   weɪ ˈbæk/
ago /əˈɡəʊ/
oh dear /əʊ ˈdɪə(r)/
we'd better . . . /wiːd
   ˈbetə(r) . . ./
the police /ðə pəˈliːs/
policewoman
   /pəˈliːswʊmən/

right /raɪt/
alone /əˈləʊn/
king /kɪŋ/
rock and roll /ˌrɒk ənd
   ˈrəʊl/
the First World War /ðə
   ˌfɜːst wɜːld ˈwɔː(r)/
champions /ˈtʃæmpɪənz/
president /ˈprezɪdənt/
space /speɪs/
the Moon /ðə ˈmuːn/
the Netherlands /ðə
   ˈneðələndz/
the Olympics /ði:
   əˈlɪmpɪks/
first /fɜːst/

walk /wɔːk/
waiter /ˈweɪtə(r)/
hotel /həʊˈtel/
cottage /ˈkɒtɪdʒ/
story /ˈstɔːrɪ/
clear /klɪə(r)/
already /ɔːlˈredɪ/
while /waɪl/
full moon /fʊl ˈmuːn/
something /ˈsʌmθɪŋ/
happen /ˈhæpən/
appear /əˈpɪə(r)/
move /muːv/
along /əˈlɒŋ/

about /ə'baʊt/
stop /stɒp/
hurry /'hʌrı/
grab /græb/
camera /'kæmrə/
return /rı'tɜ:n/
nothing /'nʌθıŋ/
sure /ʃɔ:(r)/
monster /'mɒnstə(r)/

ghost /gəʊst/
young /jʌŋ/
cry /kraı/
shout /ʃaʊt/
through /θru:/
disappear /,dısə'pıə(r)/
grey /greı/
lady /'leıdı/
a long time ago /ə lɒŋ
   ,taım ə'gəʊ/
own /əʊn/
gamble /'gæmbl/
rich /rıtʃ/
old /əʊld/
ugly /'ʌglı/
offer /'ɒfə(r)/
refuse /rı'fju:z/
marry /'mærı/
handsome /'hænsəm/
poor /pɔ:(r)/
lock /lɒk/
jump /dʒʌmp/
out of . . . /,aʊt əv '. . ./
die /daı/
fill up /fıl ʌp/
arrest /ə'rest/
leave /li:v/

UNIT 12 THE NEWS

What's going on? /wɒts
   ,gəʊıŋ 'ɒn/
alive /ə'laıv/
I bet . . . /aı bet . . ./
rat /ræt/
strange /streındʒ/
put on /pʊt ɒn/
my fault /'maı fɔ:lt/
run away /rʌn ə'weı/
you lot /'ju: lɒt/

came /keım/
had /hæd/
saw /sɔ:/
took /tʊk/
went /went/
brought /brɔ:t/
found /faʊnd/
gave /geıv/
left /left/
ran /ræn/
threw /θru:/
put /pʊt/
did /dıd/
got /gɒt/
could /kʊd/

over /'əʊvə(r)/
on his way from . . . to
   . . . /,ɒn hız weı frəm
   '. . . tə '. . ./
plane /pleın/
in the middle of . . . /ın ðə
   'mıdl əv . . ./

blew /blu:/
land /lænd/
TV studio /ti: 'vi:
   stju:dıəʊ/
interview /'ıntəvju:/
TV presenter /ti: 'vi:
   prızentə(r)/
change my mind /,tʃeındʒ
   maı 'maınd/
hit /hıt/
explode /ık'spləʊd/
fell /fel/
parachute /'pærəʃu:t/
said /sed/
snow /snəʊ/
bone /bəʊn/
break /breık/
broke /brəʊk/
heart attack /'hɑ:t ətæk/
become /bı'kʌm/
became /bı'keım/
unconscious /ʌn'kɒnʃəs/
wake up /weık 'ʌp/
woke up /wəʊk 'ʌp/
sink /sıŋk/
sank /sæŋk/
helicopter /'helıkɒptə(r)/
rescue /'reskju:/
flew /flu:/
crash /kræʃ/
caught /kɔ:t/
air stewardess /'eə
   stjʊədes/
airlines /'eəlaınz/
survive /sə'vaıv/
swam /swæm/

change /tʃeındʒ/
life /laıf/
news /nju:z/
famine /'fæmın/
famous /'feıməs/
made /meıd/
expect /ık'spekt/
feed /fi:d/
million /'mıljən/
hold /həʊld/
held /held/
medicine /'medsn/
lorry /'lɒrı/

continent /'kɒntınənt/
at the same time /,æt ðə
   seım 'taım/

UNIT 13 THE MOVIES

easily /'i:zəlı/
thought /θɔ:t/
quickly /'kwıklı/
unbutton /ʌn'bʌtn/
exciting /ık'saıtıŋ/
movies /'mu:vız/
hard /hɑ:d/
come off /kʌm 'ɒf/
turn around /tɜ:n ə'raʊnd/
push /pʊʃ/
kick /kık/
well /wel/
brave /breıv/
easy /'i:zı/
badly /'bædlı/
friendly /'frendlı/
fight /faıt/

fought /fɔ:t/
anyone /'enıwʌn/

quietly /'kwaıətlı/
loudly /'laʊdlı/
sadly /'sædlı/
slowly /'sləʊlı/

film star /'fılm stɑ:(r)/
symbol /'sımbl/
teenage rebel /,ti:neıdʒ
   'rebl/
receive /rı'si:v/
believe /bı'li:v/
dead /ded/
hero /'hıərəʊ/
people /'pi:pl/
born /bɔ:n/
farm /fɑ:m/
basketball /bɑ:skıtbɔ:l/
baseball /'beısbɔ:l/
clarinet /,klærə'net/
five years old /,faıv jıəz
   'əʊld/
go back /gəʊ 'bæk/
actor /'æktə(r)/
advertisement
   /əd'vɜ:tısmənt/
theatre /'θıətə(r)/
last /lɑ:st/
star /stɑ:(r)/
enough /ı'nʌf/
sports car /'spɔ:ts kɑ:(r)/
buy /baı/

drove /drəʊv/
bought /bɔ:t/
mph /,em pi: 'eıtʃ/
motor racing /'məʊtə
   reısıŋ/
take part in . . . /teık 'pɑ:t
   ın . . ./
race /reıs/
gold /gəʊld/
silver /'sılvə(r)/
paid /peıd/
speedometer
   /spi:'dɒmıtə(r)/
neck /nek/
legend /'ledʒənd/
bird /bɜ:d/
word /wɜ:d/
poster /'pəʊstə(r)/
Top Twenty /tɒp 'twentı/
request /rı'kwest/
navy /'neıvı/
fighter /'faıtə(r)/
top gun /tɒp 'gʌn/
fall in love /,fɔ:l ın 'lʌv/
scene /si:n/
fantastic /fæn'tæstık/
at the bottom of . . . /,æt
   ðə 'bɒtəm əv . . ./
most-requested /,məʊst
   rı'kwestıd/
since /sıns/
understand /,ʌndə'stænd/
officially /ə'fıʃəlı/
actress /'æktrıs/
part /pɑ:t/
several /'sevrəl/

UNIT 14 REVISION

murder /'mɜːdə(r)/
murderer /'mɜːdərə(r)/
bat /bæt/
dinner /'dɪnə(r)/
business partner /'bɪznɪs ˌpɑːtnə(r)/
office /'ɒfɪs/
heard /hɜːd/
floor /flɔː(r)/
French windows /ˌfrentʃ 'wɪndəʊz/

drop /drɒp/
hate /heɪt/
information /ˌɪnfə'meɪʃn/
airport /'eəpɔːt/
argument /'ɑːgjʊmənt/
fingerprints /'fɪŋgəprɪnts/
handle /'hændl/

met /met/
suspect (noun) /'sʌspekt/

USEFUL SETS

Days of the week

Monday /'mʌndɪ/
Tuesday /'tjuːzdɪ/
Wednesday /'wenzdɪ/
Thursday /'θɜːzdɪ/
Friday /'fraɪdɪ/
Saturday /'sætədɪ/
Sunday /'sʌndɪ/

Months of the year

January /'dʒænjʊərɪ/
February /'februərɪ/
March /mɑːtʃ/
April /'eɪprəl/
May /meɪ/
June /dʒuːn/
July /dʒuː'laɪ/
August /'ɔːgəst/
September /sep'tembə(r)/
October /ɒk'təʊbə(r)/
November /nəʊ'vembə(r)/
December /dɪ'sembə(r)/

Cardinal numbers

one /wʌn/
two /tuː/
three /θriː/
four /fɔː(r)/
five /faɪv/
six /sɪks/
seven /'sevn/
eight /eɪt/
nine /naɪn/
ten /ten/
eleven /ɪ'levn/
twelve /twelv/
thirteen /ˌθɜː'tiːn/
fourteen /ˌfɔː'tiːn/
fifteen /ˌfɪf'tiːn/
sixteen /ˌsɪk'stiːn/
seventeen /ˌsevn'tiːn/
eighteen /eɪ'tiːn/
nineteen /naɪn'tiːn/
twenty /'twentɪ/
twenty-one /ˌtwenti 'wʌn/
twenty-two /ˌtwenti 'tuː/
twenty-three /ˌtwenti 'θriː/
twenty-four /ˌtwenti 'fɔː(r)/
twenty-five /ˌtwenti 'faɪv/
twenty-six /ˌtwenti 'sɪks/
twenty-seven /ˌtwenti 'sevn/
twenty-eight /ˌtwenti 'aɪt/
twenty-nine /ˌtwenti 'naɪn/

thirty /'θɜːtɪ/
forty /'fɔːtɪ/
fifty /'fɪftɪ/
one hundred /wʌn 'hʌndrəd/
two hundred /tuː 'hʌndrəd/
one thousand /wʌn 'θaʊznd/
two thousand /tuː 'θaʊznd/
ten thousand /ten 'θaʊznd/
one hundred thousand /wʌn ˌhʌndrəd 'θaʊznd/
one million /wʌn 'mɪljən/

Ordinal numbers

first /fɜːst/
second /'sekənd/
third /θɜːd/
fourth /fɔːθ/
fifth /fɪfθ/
sixth /sɪksθ/
seventh /'sevnθ/
eighth /eɪtθ/
ninth /naɪnθ/
tenth /tenθ/
eleventh /ɪ'levənθ/
twelfth /twelfθ/
thirteenth /ˌθɜː'tiːnθ/
fourteenth /ˌfɔː'tiːnθ/
fifteenth /ˌfɪf'tiːnθ/
sixteenth /ˌsɪk'stiːnθ/
seventeenth /ˌsevn'tiːnθ/
eighteenth /eɪ'tiːnθ/
nineteenth /ˌnaɪn'tiːnθ/
twentieth /'twentɪəθ/
twenty-first /ˌtwenti 'fɜːst/
twenty-second /ˌtwenti 'sekənd/
twenty-third /ˌtwenti 'θɜːd/
twenty-fourth /ˌtwenti 'fɔːθ/
twenty-fifth /ˌtwenti 'fɪfθ/
twenty-sixth /ˌtwenti 'sɪksθ/
twenty-seventh /ˌtwenti 'sevənθ/
twenty-eight /ˌtwenti 'eɪtθ/
twenty-ninth /ˌtwenti 'naɪnθ/
thirtieth /'θɜːtɪəθ/
thirty-first /ˌθɜːti 'fɜːst/

Personal pronouns and adjectives

subject pronoun	object pronoun	possessive adjective
I /aɪ/	me /miː/	my /maɪ/
you /juː/	you /juː/	your /jɔː(r)/
he /hiː/	him /hɪm/	his /hɪz/
she /ʃiː/	her /hɜː(r)/	her /hɜː(r)/
it /ɪt/	it /ɪt/	its /ɪts/
we /wiː/	us /ʌs/	our /ɑː(r)/
they /ðeɪ/	them /ðem/	their /ðeə(r)/

Irregular verbs

Infinitive	Past tense
be /biː/	was /wəz/, /wɒz/
	were /wə(r)/, /wɜː(r)/
become /bɪ'kʌm/	became /bɪ'keɪm/
blow /bləʊ/	blew /bluː/
bring /brɪŋ/	brought /brɔːt/
break /breɪk/	broke /brəʊk/
buy /baɪ/	bought /bɔːt/
can /kən/, kæn/	could /kʊd/
catch /kætʃ/	caught /kɔːt/
come /kʌm/	came /keɪm/
do /də/, duː/	did /dɪd/
drive /draɪv/	drove /drəʊv/
fall /fɔːl/	fell /fel/
feed /fiːd/	fed /fed/
fight /faɪt/	fought /fɔːt/
find /faɪnd/	found /faʊnd/
fly /flaɪ/	flew /fluː/
get /get/	got /gɒt/
give /gɪv/	gave /geɪv/
go /gəʊ/	went /went/
have /hæv/	had /hæd/
have got /hæv 'gɒt/	had got /hæd 'gɒt/
hear /hɪə(r)/	heard /hɜːd/
hit /hɪt/	hit /hɪt/
hold /həʊld/	held /held/
leave /liːv/	left /left/
make /meɪk/	made /meɪd/
meet /miːt/	met /met/
pay /peɪ/	paid /peɪd/
put /pʊt/	put /pʊt/
read /riːd/	read /red/
run /rʌn/	ran /ræn/
say /seɪ/	said /sed/
see /siː/	saw /sɔː/
sink /sɪŋk/	sank /sæŋk/
take /teɪk/	took /tʊk/
think /θɪŋk/	thought /θɔːt/
throw /θrəʊ/	threw /θruː/
wake up /weɪk 'ʌp/	woke up /wəʊk 'ʌp/